Walking the Camino

Portugués

Embark on an Unforgettable Journey Through Portugal's
Historic Pilgrimage Route (Central & Coastal Route)

Anthony Morgan

Table Of Content

Introduction

The morning mist clung to Porto's ancient streets as I shouldered my backpack, its weight still unfamiliar against my shoulders. The golden scallop shell dangling from my pack caught the first rays of sunrise, marking me as one of countless pilgrims who had embarked on this ancient journey before. But this was my Camino, my Portuguese Way to Santiago de Compostela, and I had no idea how it would transform me.

The cobblestone streets of Porto gradually gave way to rural paths winding through vineyards and eucalyptus forests. The scent of salt air from the Atlantic mingled with the earthiness of countryside, creating an intoxicating perfume that would become the signature fragrance of my journey. Each step took me further from the familiar and deeper into a world where time seemed to move at the pace of footsteps rather than clock hands.

On my third day, I met Maria, an 80-year-old Portuguese woman who had walked this route seven times. She didn't speak English, and my Portuguese was limited to "obrigado" and "bom dia," but somehow we shared a deep conversation through gestures, smiles, and the universal language of kindness. She pressed a handful of fresh figs into my palm before our paths diverged – a simple gift that tasted sweeter than any luxury dessert.

The rhythm of pilgrim life quickly became my new normal. Wake at dawn, pack light, walk far. My feet developed their own wisdom, and my mind learned to quiet itself in the meditation of movement. Sometimes I walked alone for hours, counting steps or listening to the whispers of wind through cornfields. Other times, I fell into step with fellow pilgrims – a German architect searching for inspiration, a Brazilian woman walking through grief, a young Spanish couple celebrating their engagement.

The albergues (pilgrim hostels) became nightly theaters of human connection. In one memorable evening in Ponte de Lima, a dozen of us from eight different countries shared a communal meal of caldo verde soup and vinho verde wine. Someone produced a guitar, and soon the ancient stone walls echoed with songs in multiple languages. Our blistered feet and aching muscles were forgotten in the warmth of newfound friendship.

Not every moment was poetic. There were days of relentless rain when my waterproof gear proved anything but. My feet rebelled with angry blisters, and once I got hopelessly lost in an industrial zone outside Valença. Yet even these challenges became part of the pilgrimage's gifts, teaching me patience, resilience, and the art of asking for help.

The landscape told its own story as I crossed from Portugal into Spain. Medieval bridges arched over rushing rivers, ancient churches offered cool sanctuary from afternoon heat, and mysterious petroglyphs whispered tales of those who had passed this way thousands of years before. Each village brought new discoveries – a tiny café serving the world's best pastel de nata, a forgotten Romanesque chapel with fading frescoes, an elderly man tending his garden who insisted on filling my water bottle with homemade wine.

As I approached Santiago de Compostela, something shifted. The anticipation of reaching the famous cathedral was strong, but I found myself walking more slowly, savoring each moment. I had learned that the true magic of the Camino lies not in the destination but in the journey itself – in the conversations with strangers who become friends, in the solitary moments of reflection, in the simple joy of moving through a landscape step by step.

When I finally arrived in Santiago's grand plaza, tears surprised me. They weren't tears of triumph or relief, but of gratitude for every step that had brought me here. The cathedral's towers soared above me, but my eyes were drawn to a fellow pilgrim

I'd met days ago, now rushing to embrace me like a long-lost friend. We had arrived, yes, but the real gift was everything that had happened in between.

My Camino Portugués taught me that the most profound journeys happen both on the outside and the inside. Like countless pilgrims before me, I had come seeking something – adventure, perhaps, or clarity. What I found was a deeper understanding of simplicity, connection, and the extraordinary magic hidden within ordinary moments. The Way had changed me, step by step, smile by smile, one story at a time.

Chapter 1

Welcome to the Camino Portugués

There's something magical about setting out on foot, following in the steps of centuries-old pilgrims, letting the rhythm of your footsteps guide you through landscapes that feel timeless. The Camino Portugués offers just that—an experience that blends history, nature, and personal reflection into a single journey. Whether you're seeking a deep spiritual experience or just want to walk through some of the most beautiful regions of Portugal and Spain, the Camino Portugués has a unique way of drawing people in.

This route, beginning in Portugal and winding its way north into Spain, is the second most popular path to Santiago de Compostela, after the Camino Francés. Along the way, you'll find welcoming towns, stunning coastlines, lush forests, and a sense of connection not just to the land but to the countless pilgrims who've walked this way before you.

Overview of the Camino Portugués

The Camino Portugués offers a gentler experience compared to some other Camino routes. With its mix of peaceful countryside, charming towns, and scenic coastlines, it is a path of quiet beauty. While the pilgrimage has deep religious roots, you don't need to be driven by faith to appreciate what this journey brings. It's a chance to slow down, reflect, and enjoy the simplicity of walking.

This Camino begins in Lisbon for the truly adventurous, but most walkers start in Porto, famous for its historic riverside and port wine. From there, you have two main paths to choose from: the Central Route, which takes you inland through traditional towns and forests, or the Coastal Route, where the sound of the Atlantic waves will accompany your steps.

Each variant has its charm, and whichever path you choose, you'll end up in Santiago de Compostela, the city where pilgrims have gathered for over a thousand years to pay homage to the Apostle St. James.

History and Significance of the Route

The Camino Portugués has been a pilgrimage route since the Middle Ages. As early as the 12th century, pilgrims from Portugal would journey north to Santiago de Compostela, seeking spiritual guidance, healing, or to give thanks. The route itself traces the rich cultural exchange between Portugal and Spain, and walking it today still carries that same sense of crossing through history.

You'll pass Roman bridges, medieval churches, and ancient towns where pilgrims once rested, prayed, and sought solace. Along the way, you'll also see the quiet remnants of centuries of devotion: simple stone crosses, pilgrim's shelters, and chapels tucked into the landscape.

But even for those who don't walk with religious intent, the Camino Portugués offers a powerful sense of continuity, connecting you to the footsteps of countless others who sought something more, whether spiritual, personal, or just a deeper connection to the world around them.

Choosing Between the Central and Coastal Routes

One of the great things about the Camino Portugués is the choice it gives you between two distinct routes, both starting from Porto: the Central Route and the Coastal Route.

- **The Central Route** is the more traditional path, leading you through the heart of Portugal and Galicia. This path takes you through ancient towns, across rolling hills, and past vineyards and forests. The landscape is varied, with plenty of historical and cultural highlights along the way. If you're looking for a more classic pilgrimage experience, this might be your route.

- **The Coastal Route,** on the other hand, offers the stunning beauty of the Atlantic Ocean as your walking companion. Starting from Porto, it follows Portugal's northern coastline before turning inland toward Santiago. This path is often breezier and cooler than the Central Route, with fewer steep climbs. It's perfect for those who love being near the sea and want to experience a quieter Camino, as it's less crowded than the Central Route.

Both routes converge near the Spanish town of Redondela, so no matter which path you choose, you'll end up sharing the final stages with other pilgrims. It's not uncommon for some to start on one route and switch to the other, depending on their mood or the weather.

Who Should Walk the Camino Portugués?

The Camino Portugués is for anyone who feels the pull of the Camino but perhaps seeks something a bit quieter than the Camino Francés. If you're drawn to history, love scenic walks, or simply need space to think, this route is an ideal choice. You don't have to be in top physical condition, as the terrain is generally kinder than other routes. It's more about endurance and enjoying the journey.

This route is also perfect for those who want a more intimate Camino experience. You won't find the same crowds as on the Camino Francés, which means more time to reflect, fewer packed albergues, and a deeper sense of connection with fellow pilgrims.

If you appreciate a balance of countryside, culture, and coastline, the Camino Portugués offers a bit of everything. And while it's certainly a physical challenge, the path is forgiving enough for those walking their first Camino. Whether you're walking to reconnect with yourself, find spiritual meaning, or just see the world at a different pace, the Camino Portugués welcomes everyone, no matter their reason

Chapter 2

Planning Your Camino Portugués

Embarking on the Camino Portugués is an exciting prospect, but like any great journey, it requires some thoughtful planning. Whether you're aiming for the Central Route, the Coastal Route, or a mix of both, understanding the best time to walk and how long it will take is key to making your experience memorable, enjoyable, and manageable. Here's a breakdown to help you prepare with confidence.

When to Walk

Choosing the right time to walk the Camino can make all the difference between a pleasant, life-affirming experience and one that feels like you're battling the elements. The Camino Portugués is walkable year-round, but each season offers something different. Here's a guide to help you decide what suits your preferences and needs.

Best Time of Year

- **Spring (April to June):** Spring is often considered the best time to walk the Camino Portugués. The weather is mild, the landscape is lush and green, and flowers bloom all around. This season offers comfortable walking temperatures, with fewer rainy days than autumn. It's also before the peak of the summer heat, which can be a blessing, especially if you're not accustomed to long walks in high temperatures.

- **Summer (July to August):** If you love sunny days and warm evenings, summer could be ideal for you, but be prepared for some challenges. The heat, particularly on the Central Route, can be intense, with temperatures often rising above 30°C (86°F) in the afternoons. You'll need to start early to avoid walking in the heat of the day. That said, this is the time when you'll meet the most pilgrims, which can bring a lively social aspect to your journey.

- **Autumn (September to October):** The cooler, crisper air of autumn makes for another excellent time to walk. The crowds from the summer months start to thin out, and the landscape, particularly along the Coastal Route, takes on a golden hue. September can still be warm, while October brings cooler temperatures and the possibility of rain, but nothing that should deter you if you're properly prepared.

- **Winter (November to March):** Winter is the quietest time on the Camino, which can appeal to those seeking solitude. However, it comes with challenges. The weather can be unpredictable—expect rain, cold, and possibly snow in some parts of northern Spain. Many albergues (pilgrim hostels) close during the winter months, so accommodations can be sparse. If you do decide to walk during this season, it's essential to be well-prepared for wet, cold conditions, and have a flexible plan in place.

Weather Considerations for Central and Coastal Routes

- **Central Route**: This inland path tends to be warmer, especially in the summer. Spring and autumn provide the most comfortable conditions. If walking in summer, early starts and afternoon breaks in shaded spots are key to avoiding the midday heat. Rain can be common in autumn, but it's generally mild.

- **Coastal Route**: As expected, the Coastal Route benefits from the cool Atlantic breezes, making it a refreshing option during the summer months. The temperatures are more moderate here compared to the Central Route, but the trade-off is that the coastal weather can be unpredictable, with a higher chance of rain, particularly in spring and autumn. If you love the ocean, this route offers an incredible balance between nature and climate.

Avoiding Crowds: Off-Season vs. High-Season

- **High-Season (June to September):** The Camino sees its highest number of pilgrims during the summer months, especially in July and August. The upside is the abundance of open albergues and a strong sense of camaraderie, but this also means busier paths, packed accommodations, and less quiet time for reflection. If you don't mind the company and prefer guaranteed facilities being open, this is your time.

- **Off-Season (October to March):** Walking during the quieter months offers peace and a chance for deeper reflection, but you'll face fewer open albergues, colder weather, and potentially tricky conditions. If you're someone who prefers solitude and doesn't mind the cooler air, early autumn and late spring provide a nice balance between quiet and comfort.

How Long Will It Take?

The Camino Portugués offers a range of starting points and routes, so how long it takes depends on where you begin and which path you choose. Whether you're walking from Lisbon, Porto, or even starting closer to Santiago, you'll want to consider your pace, your fitness level, and how much time you can dedicate to the journey.

Time Estimates for Each Route (Central and Coastal)

- **Central Route from Lisbon (610 km):** Starting from Lisbon means committing to a full month of walking, typically 4-6 weeks depending on your pace. This route is less traveled until you reach Porto, offering a quieter experience through central Portugal.

- **Central Route from Porto (240 km):** Porto is a popular starting point, and from here, the journey to Santiago de Compostela typically takes 10-14 days, depending on your pace and how many rest days you plan to take. The terrain is moderate, and you'll find a well-developed network of albergues.

- **Coastal Route from Porto (260 km):** The Coastal Route also takes around 10-14 days from Porto to Santiago, though many pilgrims find it slightly easier thanks to its flatter terrain. The seaside views are a stunning bonus, but the weather can be more unpredictable. Some days might involve shorter distances due to rain or strong winds along the coast.

Customizing Your Journey Based on Time and Fitness Levels

- **For 2-Week Walkers**: If you have around two weeks, Porto is the perfect starting point. Both the Central and Coastal routes can be completed within this time frame, with daily walking distances ranging from 20 to 30 kilometers. If you're not in a rush, you can add a few rest days to explore towns like Pontevedra, Valença, or the coastal charm of Baiona.

- **For 1-Week Walkers**: If you only have a week, starting in Tui (just across the Portuguese border) is a great option. From here, the distance to Santiago is about 100 kilometers, the minimum needed to receive your Compostela. This shorter route can be completed in 5-7 days, perfect for those on a tighter schedule.

- For Slower Paced Pilgrims or Those with More Time: If you prefer a slower pace or simply want to savor the journey, walking from Lisbon will give you the full experience. You can break your days into shorter, more manageable distances, taking time to rest and explore the many historical towns along the way. This extended journey is ideal for those looking to fully immerse themselves in the Camino spirit.

In the end, how long the Camino takes depends on your priorities. Some walk quickly, pushing themselves physically, while others take it slow, absorbing the sights, sounds, and moments of reflection. There is no right or wrong way—only your way.

What to Pack

Packing for the Camino Portugués can feel like a bit of a balancing act. You want to be prepared for everything the journey might throw at you, but you also don't want to lug around a heavy backpack for hundreds of kilometers. The key is finding that sweet spot where you have everything you need but nothing more. Remember, your pack will become your constant companion, so keeping it light and practical will make your Camino far more enjoyable.

Essential Gear and Equipment

Your backpack is arguably the most important piece of gear you'll bring on the Camino. A well-fitted pack can make or break your experience. Look for something in the 30-40 liter range. That's big enough to hold everything you need but small enough to encourage you not to overpack. Make sure it has comfortable, padded shoulder straps and a waist belt to help distribute the weight.

Here's a list of essential gear you shouldn't leave home without:

- **Comfortable Backpack (30-40 liters):** Invest in a good one with a rain cover.

- **Sleeping Bag or Sleep Sack**: Depending on the season, a lightweight sleeping bag or sleep sack is usually sufficient for most pilgrim accommodations. Some albergues provide blankets, but you won't want to rely on that.

- **Water Bottle or Hydration System**: Staying hydrated is crucial, especially on hot days. A 1-2 liter bottle should be fine, or you can use a hydration bladder for easy access while walking.

- **Trekking Poles (optional)**: These aren't for everyone, but they can take some pressure off your knees, especially on steep descents. If you're unsure, it's worth trying them out on a practice hike before you leave.

- **Poncho or Rain Jacket:** The weather can change quickly, especially in Galicia, so you'll want something to keep you dry during unexpected showers.

- **Guidebook or Map:** Though the Camino Portugués is well-marked, a guidebook with maps can be helpful for planning your stages, learning about towns along the way, and tracking your progress.

Clothing Recommendations

When it comes to clothing, versatility is key. You want lightweight, moisture-wicking materials that can be layered for warmth and comfort. You'll also be doing laundry along the way, so don't pack too much. Two sets of clothes (one for walking, one for relaxing in the evenings) should be plenty.

Here are some clothing essentials to consider:

- **Moisture-Wicking Shirts (2-3):** These are your base layers. Look for synthetic or merino wool fabrics that dry quickly and keep sweat away from your skin.
- **Lightweight Pants/Shorts (1-2 pairs):** Zip-off hiking pants that convert to shorts are great for fluctuating temperatures. Avoid heavy fabrics like denim.
- **Socks (2-3 pairs):** Invest in good-quality hiking socks that provide cushioning and prevent blisters. Some pilgrims swear by liner socks for extra protection.
- **Underwear (2-3 pairs):** Again, lightweight, quick-drying materials are best.
- **Light Fleece or Sweater:** Mornings and evenings can be chilly, even in summer.
- **Hat and Sunglasses:** You'll be out in the sun a lot, so protect yourself from the heat.
- **Walking Shoes or Boots:** Choose footwear that's already broken in and provides good support. Some prefer lightweight hiking boots, while others go for trail shoes. The most important thing is comfort.
- **Sandals or Flip-Flops:** These are great for giving your feet a break in the evenings and wearing in the showers.

You'll be wearing the same clothes day in and day out, so don't worry too much about looking stylish. Comfort and practicality should be your guiding principles here.

Packing Light: Tips and Tricks

Keeping your pack light is all about smart choices. Here are some tips that can make a big difference:

- **Stick to the Rule of Two**: Two shirts, two pairs of socks, two pairs of underwear—one to wear, one to wash. With laundromats and sinks available along the way, you don't need more than that.

- **Use Travel-Sized Toiletries**: Don't bring full-sized bottles of shampoo and soap. Buy travel-sized containers or even better, switch to solid soap and shampoo bars—they're lighter and won't leak.

- **Multi-Purpose Items**: Choose gear that serves multiple purposes. For example, a sarong can be used as a towel, a blanket, or even a makeshift curtain in dorm rooms. A buff can double as a headband or a neck warmer.

- **Limit Electronics**: While it's tempting to bring all your gadgets, they can add unnecessary weight. A smartphone, power bank, and charger should cover most needs. If you want to document your journey, consider a lightweight camera instead of a bulky DSLR.

- **Resupply Along the Way**: You don't need to pack enough toiletries or snacks for the entire trip. There are plenty of shops along the Camino, so you can restock as needed.

Every extra pound on your back will feel like five by the end of a long day. Be honest with yourself—if you don't absolutely need it, leave it behind.

First Aid Kit and Health Essentials

A well-prepared first aid kit can save you a lot of discomfort along the Camino. Blisters are the most common ailment among pilgrims, so your kit should be stocked to deal with them, as well as other minor injuries or illnesses.

Here's a basic first aid kit to bring along:

- **Blister Care Supplies**: Compeed or other blister plasters are a must. Include antiseptic wipes, bandages, and tape to help prevent or treat hotspots.
- **Pain Relievers**: Ibuprofen or paracetamol can help with sore muscles and minor aches after a long day of walking.
- **Anti-Chafing Cream**: Some pilgrims swear by BodyGlide or Vaseline to prevent chafing, especially in areas where your pack or clothing rubs.

- **Foot Powder**: Keeping your feet dry can help prevent blisters and athlete's foot.

- **Rehydration Tablets**: These can be a lifesaver on hot days or after a stomach bug.

- **Sunblock and Lip Balm**: Protect yourself from sunburn, even on cloudy days.

- **Insect Repellent**: In the warmer months, mosquitoes can be a nuisance, especially on the Coastal Route.

- **Prescription Medications**: Make sure you have enough of any prescription medications to last the trip, as you may not be able to easily refill them on the Camino.

The goal is to be prepared without overpacking. You can always find a pharmacy along the route if you need something more specific.

Packing for the Camino Portugués is about striking the right balance between comfort and practicality. You'll be surprised by how little you actually need, and there's something liberating about traveling light. Every item in your pack should serve a purpose, and the lighter you pack, the more you'll enjoy the journey. After all, the Camino is as much about what you leave behind as it is about what you bring with you.

Chapter 3

Getting There/Starting Point

Lisbon

For many pilgrims embarking on the Camino Portugués, Lisbon serves as the gateway to this remarkable journey northward to Santiago de Compostela. Lisbon, Portugal's bustling capital, is a city filled with history, charm, and modern vibrance, offering the perfect setting to begin a pilgrimage that will take you through stunning landscapes, historic villages, and sacred sites. Starting your Camino from Lisbon adds a sense of completeness to the experience, allowing you to walk from one great cultural and spiritual hub to another.

Arriving in Lisbon

Getting to Lisbon is relatively easy, as the city is well-connected by air, train, and bus routes from across Europe and beyond. Lisbon Portela Airport (LIS) is the main international gateway, receiving flights from most major cities. From the airport, you can quickly reach the city center by metro, bus, or taxi, making it a convenient arrival point for pilgrims from all over the world.

If you're already in Portugal or coming from Spain, Lisbon is also accessible by train, with regular services from Porto, Coimbra, and Faro, as well as from Madrid. The city's Oriente

Station is the primary hub for long-distance trains, while Santa Apolónia Station serves regional and international routes.

Once in Lisbon, take a day or two to explore this vibrant city before setting out on your pilgrimage. The city itself feels like a prologue to the journey, full of winding streets, terracotta rooftops, and breathtaking views from places like the Miradouro de Santa Catarina or the Belém Tower. It's a chance to ground yourself before taking the first steps toward Santiago.

Why Start from Lisbon?

Many pilgrims choose to begin their Camino Portugués from Porto or even from the Spanish border, but starting from Lisbon adds a deeper, more immersive dimension to your journey. Walking from Lisbon means covering nearly 620 kilometers (385 miles) over several weeks. It's a significant commitment, but one that offers a richer, more varied experience.

Starting from Lisbon allows you to experience the full scope of the Portuguese countryside and its evolving landscapes. The first few days out of Lisbon will take you through urban and industrial areas, but soon enough, the route opens up into peaceful villages, lush vineyards, and rolling hills. It's a path that reveals the diversity of Portugal, from the hustle and bustle of the capital to the quiet serenity of its rural heartland.

There's also something symbolic about starting in Lisbon. This city has been a point of departure for explorers, adventurers, and pilgrims for centuries. As you walk out of its boundaries, you join in a long tradition of seekers leaving behind the known to venture toward something greater.

Challenges of Starting from Lisbon

While the Camino from Lisbon offers a rewarding experience, it's important to acknowledge some of the challenges. The route from Lisbon is less traveled compared to the sections starting from Porto, which means fewer pilgrims, fewer albergues (pilgrim hostels), and fewer services along the way. The path is well-marked, but the distances between accommodations can be longer, especially in the early stages. This requires more planning, particularly in terms of where to sleep and where to stock up on food and water.

The terrain from Lisbon is relatively flat, but the urban and industrial areas during the first few days can be less picturesque than the rural landscapes that follow. Some pilgrims find these initial stages a bit monotonous, but they also offer a good opportunity to ease into the pilgrimage, both mentally and physically. It's a gradual build-up, and before long, the scenery transforms into the rolling hills and vineyards that make this route so beloved.

Starting in Lisbon is also a commitment to a longer Camino, and it's important to be prepared for the physical endurance required. The total distance from Lisbon to Santiago is over 600 kilometers, typically taking about 30 to 35 days to complete. If you're new to long-distance walking, it's wise to build up your fitness before beginning the journey.

Final Thoughts on Starting from Lisbon

Beginning your Camino from Lisbon adds a unique depth to your pilgrimage. It's not the easiest or the quickest option, but it offers an incredibly rich experience—both culturally and personally. You'll have time to fully immerse yourself in the rhythm of the Camino, with each step taking you further into the heart of Portugal and closer to your ultimate goal in Santiago de Compostela.

Whether you're walking for spiritual reasons, personal reflection, or simply to experience the beauty of the landscape, starting in Lisbon allows you to fully embrace the journey. It's a path less traveled, offering moments of quiet solitude, unexpected challenges, and profound connections with both the land and your fellow pilgrims.

As with all Caminos, it's not just about reaching Santiago, but about the journey itself. And from Lisbon, that journey is as varied and enriching as the land it passes through.

Porto

Porto, Portugal's second-largest city, is not only famous for its scenic riverside, historic architecture, and world-renowned port wine, but it also serves as one of the most popular starting points for pilgrims walking the Camino Portugués. For many, Porto is where the real adventure begins, offering a blend of urban exploration and the first taste of the road ahead. Whether you're flying directly into Porto or arriving by train, this city marks the beginning of your journey to Santiago de Compostela.

Why Start in Porto?

Though the Camino Portugués officially begins in Lisbon, many pilgrims choose to start in Porto for a number of practical and scenic reasons. First, starting your pilgrimage from Lisbon adds roughly 250 kilometers to the journey, which can be too long for those on a time constraint or those seeking a shorter, more manageable walk. The route from Porto is around 240 kilometers to Santiago, making it the perfect starting point for a two-week journey, which is ideal for most first-time pilgrims.

Porto also offers two beautiful and distinct paths: the Central Route and the Coastal Route, giving you the freedom to tailor your Camino experience based on your preferences.

Getting to Porto

Getting to Porto is relatively easy, with plenty of options depending on where you're coming from.

- **By Air**: Porto's international airport, Francisco Sá Carneiro Airport (OPO), is well-connected to major cities across Europe and even some long-haul destinations. There are direct flights from hubs like London, Paris, Frankfurt, and Madrid. From the airport, getting into the city center is straightforward—you can take the metro, bus, or taxi.

- **By Train**: If you're already in Portugal or traveling from Spain, taking the train to Porto can be a scenic and relaxing option. Campanhã Station is Porto's main rail hub, offering frequent trains from Lisbon (a journey of about 3 hours) and from the Spanish cities of Vigo or Madrid. From Campanhã, it's just a quick metro or bus ride into Porto's city center.

- **By Bus**: Several bus companies connect Porto with other cities in Portugal and Spain. Buses are often a cheaper option than trains, though the journeys can be longer. Popular bus companies like Rede Expressos and ALSA offer regular services to Porto.

- **By Car**: If you prefer to drive, major highways connect Porto to other parts of Portugal and Spain. However, parking in the city can be challenging, and you likely won't need a car once your pilgrimage begins.

Starting the Camino from Porto

Once you've arrived in Porto, you'll find yourself in a city brimming with history, culture, and charm. Before setting out on your pilgrimage, it's worth taking some time to explore Porto's cobbled streets, riverfront views, and iconic landmarks. Many pilgrims spend a day or two in Porto, soaking in the atmosphere before hitting the road. Key spots to visit include:

- **Ribeira District**: The city's riverside area, with its colorful buildings, bustling cafes, and stunning views of the Douro River, is a perfect place to start your pilgrimage mentally. Walking along the Ribeira feels like a prelude to the journey ahead.
- **São Bento Train Station:** Famous for its beautiful azulejo tile work, São Bento is a must-see for any visitor. The historic station also symbolizes the idea of starting a journey, as trains to and from Porto have been departing from here since the 19th century.

- **Port Wine Cellars**: While you'll need to be careful not to overindulge before starting your pilgrimage, Porto's famous wine cellars are worth a visit. Located across the river in Vila Nova de Gaia, they offer guided tours and tastings.

After exploring the city and preparing for the walk ahead, it's time to officially start the Camino. You'll find the first markers of the Camino Portugués within the city, typically represented by yellow arrows or the scallop shell, the symbol of the pilgrimage to Santiago. From Porto, you have two primary routes to choose from:

The Central Route

The Central Route is the traditional inland path of the Camino Portugués, leading north from Porto through a mix of urban areas, rural countryside, and historical towns. This route is more popular among pilgrims because it passes through charming Portuguese villages like Barcelos, famous for its pottery and the legendary Rooster of Barcelos, and Ponte de Lima, one of the oldest towns in Portugal with its beautiful Roman bridge.

The terrain on the Central Route is varied, offering gentle hills, farmlands, and shaded forests. Along the way, you'll find plenty of albergues (pilgrim hostels) and small cafés to rest and refuel. The route also has a rich historical and cultural significance, passing by numerous churches, monasteries, and medieval landmarks.

Highlights of the Central Route:
- The medieval town of Barcelos, known for its historic significance and vibrant local culture.
- Ponte de Lima, the oldest town in Portugal, with its stunning Roman bridge and peaceful riverbanks.
- The lush green countryside of northern Portugal, offering a serene walking experience through vineyards and farmlands.

The Coastal Route

The Coastal Route (Caminho da Costa) offers a completely different experience, as it hugs Portugal's northern coastline, taking you past beautiful beaches, fishing villages, and dramatic Atlantic views. This route is perfect for those who love the sound of the ocean as their walking companion and prefer a cooler, breezier path.

Leaving Porto, you'll walk along the coast to towns like Vila do Conde and Esposende, before crossing into Spain. The coastal breeze and flat terrain make this a more leisurely walk, though it's slightly longer than the Central Route.

Highlights of the Coastal Route:
- Walking along the Atlantic Ocean, with breathtaking sea views.
- The charming fishing village of Vila do Conde, known for its long sandy beaches and historic shipbuilding heritage.
- The tranquil, quiet paths away from the inland crowds, making it a more reflective and peaceful experience for many.

Practical Tips for Starting in Porto

- **Pick Up Your Credencial**: Before setting off, make sure you have your Credencial del Peregrino, or pilgrim passport, which you'll need to collect stamps along the way. In Porto, you can pick one up at the Cathedral of Porto (Sé do Porto) or at the Igreja de Santo António dos Congregados.
- **Footwear Check:** Porto's streets are cobbled and sometimes uneven, making it a good place to test your shoes before heading off on longer paths. Make sure they're comfortable and well broken-in to avoid blisters later.
- **Take It Easy**: The first day's walk out of Porto can feel long, especially if you're still adjusting to the weight of your

backpack. Don't rush—pace yourself, and enjoy the beginning of what will be a life-changing journey.

Starting the Camino Portugués in Porto offers the perfect blend of urban vibrancy and the calm that comes with setting out on a pilgrimage. From here, the road to Santiago stretches ahead, full of potential, adventure, and personal discovery. Porto, with its rich history and stunning landscapes, is the ideal place to start your journey—whether you're walking for spiritual reasons or simply seeking a memorable experience on one of the world's most famous pilgrimage routes.

Tui

The Camino Portugués offers several starting points depending on how long you'd like your pilgrimage to be, but one of the most popular and convenient spots to begin is Tui, a charming town located right on the border between Portugal and Spain. Tui marks the beginning of the last 100 kilometers of the Camino Portugués, the minimum distance required to earn the coveted Compostela certificate upon arrival in Santiago de Compostela.

Whether you're traveling from abroad or already within Spain or Portugal, getting to Tui is relatively easy, and its location along the Río Miño makes for a scenic and memorable starting point for your Camino.

Why Start in Tui?

Tui is an ideal starting point for pilgrims who want to walk a manageable yet meaningful distance to Santiago de Compostela. At approximately 115 kilometers from Santiago, it offers a balanced experience—enough time to immerse yourself in the rhythm of the Camino but not so long that it feels overwhelming, especially for first-time pilgrims.

As a small but historically rich town, Tui offers a great introduction to what's to come along the Camino Portugués. The town's well-preserved medieval core, stunning views across the Miño River into Portugal, and welcoming pilgrim infrastructure make it a comfortable and inspiring place to begin your journey. Plus, because of its proximity to Santiago, starting in Tui guarantees you'll walk through some of Galicia's most beautiful landscapes, with rolling green hills, stone villages, and ancient woodlands guiding you toward your final destination.

Getting to Tui: Travel Options

By Air:

The closest major airport to Tui is Vigo Airport (VGO), located about 25 kilometers away. From Vigo, you can catch a bus or a taxi to Tui. Alternatively, Porto Airport (OPO) in

Portugal is roughly 120 kilometers from Tui, and many pilgrims choose to fly into Porto for its larger range of international flights. From Porto, you can take a train, bus, or car to Tui, crossing the border into Spain.

By Train:

Trains are a great way to reach Tui, especially if you're already in Spain or Portugal. From Vigo, there are frequent regional trains that take you to Guillarei, the nearest train station to Tui. Guillarei is just a short taxi or bus ride (about 3 kilometers) from Tui's town center.

If you're coming from further south in Portugal, you can take a train from Porto to the Portuguese town of Valença, which lies directly across the river from Tui. It's an easy walk across the international bridge over the Miño River to reach Tui from Valença, and the crossing itself is a symbolic and exciting way to start your pilgrimage.

By Bus:

Buses also serve Tui from major cities like Vigo, Santiago de Compostela, and Porto. The bus is usually the most cost-effective option, especially for pilgrims traveling on a budget. The journey from Vigo to Tui takes about an hour, and from Porto, it's roughly two hours. Bus services in the area are reliable, and many buses are geared toward pilgrims, making it easy to find routes that connect you to Tui.

By Car:

If you prefer the flexibility of traveling by car, driving to Tui is straightforward. The AP-9 motorway connects Vigo to Tui, and the drive takes just under 30 minutes. From Porto, you'll follow the A3 motorway north to Valença, and from there, it's only a few minutes across the bridge into Spain and Tui. While you won't need a car once you begin walking, you can park in Tui and arrange for a service to transfer your vehicle to Santiago, or you can simply rely on public transport once you complete your Camino.

What to Expect in Tui

Upon arriving in Tui, you'll find yourself immersed in a town with deep historical significance and a palpable sense of pilgrimage. Tui has been a gateway for pilgrims entering Spain for centuries, and its ancient streets and stone buildings reflect that rich heritage.

One of the must-see landmarks in Tui is the Tui Cathedral, a striking combination of Romanesque and Gothic architecture, which looms over the town's historic center. Pilgrims often visit the cathedral before setting out on their journey, lighting a candle or saying a prayer for protection and guidance. The cathedral's fortress-like appearance and beautiful interior provide a fitting backdrop for the start of your pilgrimage.

As you wander through Tui's narrow, cobbled streets, you'll come across various cafes, restaurants, and small shops catering to pilgrims. It's a good idea to stock up on any last-minute supplies here, from snacks and water bottles to walking poles and blister care items. Tui has a number of albergues (pilgrim hostels) and small hotels, so if you arrive the day before you plan to start walking, you'll find plenty of accommodation options.

Starting in Tui offers a perfect balance for pilgrims seeking a taste of the Camino without committing to a longer, more strenuous journey. It's an accessible starting point, rich with history and culture, and it allows you to experience the heart of Galicia as you make your way toward Santiago de Compostela. Whether you arrive by train, plane, or bus, starting your Camino in Tui promises a journey filled with beauty, reflection, and the camaraderie of fellow travelers all walking toward the same sacred destination.

Chapter 4

The Central Route (Lisbon to Santiago)

Stage 1 - Stage 7

Lisbon to Alverca do Ribatejo

The Central Route of the Camino Portugués starts in Lisbon, a city bursting with culture, history, and charm. From its picturesque streets to the grand monuments, Lisbon offers a lively start to your pilgrimage. The journey from Lisbon to Alverca do Ribatejo covers roughly 23 kilometers, making it a great introductory day on the Camino. Though this first stage may feel more urban than rural, it's a nice warm-up for the long roads ahead, easing you into the rhythm of the pilgrimage.

Lisbon: A City of Discoveries

Before you take your first steps, Lisbon deserves at least a day or two to explore. The city is a blend of ancient history and modern vibrancy. It's known for its iconic Belém Tower, the intricate details of the Jerónimos Monastery, and the lively neighborhoods of Bairro Alto and Alfama. Take a stroll down the cobblestone streets, enjoy the views from one of Lisbon's many miradouros (viewpoints), and make sure to try the city's famous custard tarts, Pastéis de Nata, at Pastéis de Belém.

If you're looking for a good night's sleep before your Camino begins, Lisbon offers plenty of accommodation options to suit various budgets.

- Hotel Recommendations:
- **Hotel My Story Rossio**: This boutique hotel in the heart of Lisbon is close to many landmarks and offers a comfortable stay with modern amenities. Its central location is perfect for exploring the city before your Camino.

- **Lisbon Poets Hostel**: For those on a budget, this cozy and friendly hostel in the Chiado district offers dorms and private rooms. It's a great spot to meet other travelers and share stories before starting your pilgrimage.

After a restful night, indulge in a hearty breakfast—Café A Brasileira is a local favorite—before setting off on your journey north.

The Road from Lisbon to Alverca do Ribatejo

As you leave the city behind, the route from Lisbon to Alverca do Ribatejo follows mostly paved roads, passing through some industrial areas and suburbs. Though this part of the Camino may not have the rural charm of later stages, it offers glimpses into everyday Portuguese life. You'll pass local shops, schools, and homes as you make your way out of the metropolitan area.

The Camino markers in Lisbon are well maintained, but keep an eye out for the yellow arrows as you navigate your way through the city's outskirts. It's not uncommon to miss a marker or two, especially in busier areas, so having a map or GPS app handy can be helpful.

Around midday, you'll find yourself walking along the Tagus River, offering a refreshing view as you head toward Alverca. This flat, scenic stretch provides a nice break from the more urban environment. You might pass fellow pilgrims or even locals out for a jog along the riverbank.

Arriving in Alverca do Ribatejo

After about 23 kilometers, you'll arrive in Alverca do Ribatejo, a quieter town just north of Lisbon. It's not a major tourist destination, but it's a practical stop with a few places to rest and recharge after your first day on the Camino.

Alverca is known for its Aviation Museum, which offers an interesting diversion for history buffs and aviation enthusiasts. Even if planes aren't your passion, it's a unique stop to break up the journey.

- Hotel Recommendations:
  - **VIP Executive Santa Iria Hotel**: Located just a short distance from Alverca, this comfortable hotel offers all the basic amenities you'll need for a good night's rest. It's perfect if you want something a bit more upscale before heading into more rural parts of the Camino.

- **Residencial Vila Verde:** For a more budget-friendly option, this guesthouse provides clean, simple rooms and a welcoming atmosphere. It's a good choice for pilgrims looking for a no-frills stay at the end of the first day.

Where to Eat in Alverca do Ribatejo

After a day of walking, finding a good meal is essential. While Alverca may not have the range of dining options that Lisbon offers, you can still enjoy a satisfying, hearty meal at one of the local spots.

- Restaurant Recommendations:

- **Restaurante O Mercado**: This cozy, family-run restaurant is known for its generous portions and delicious Portuguese cuisine. Try their bacalhau à brás (a traditional salted cod dish) or a simple bifana (pork sandwich) for a filling meal.

- **Café o Telheiro:** If you're looking for something lighter or just a snack, this café offers a range of sandwiches, pastries, and coffee. It's a great place to relax and people-watch after a day on your feet.

The Pilgrim Spirit

Your first day on the Camino might not be filled with rolling hills or ancient villages, but it serves as an important introduction to the pilgrimage. It's a day to find your pace, get used to the weight of your backpack, and start adjusting to the mindset of a pilgrim. The urban start can be challenging for some, but remember that the Camino is as much about the inner journey as it is about the physical one. As you walk, take time to reflect on why you're here and what you hope to find on this path.

By the time you reach Alverca do Ribatejo, you'll have a better sense of the Camino's rhythm. You'll have felt the soreness in your muscles, the peace that comes with walking, and maybe even had your first meaningful conversation with a fellow pilgrim. This is just the beginning—tomorrow, the road opens up, and you'll begin to see the Portugal of rolling vineyards, ancient towns, and quiet trails that the Camino is known for.

For now, rest your feet, enjoy a good meal, and take in the sense of accomplishment that comes with completing your first stage. Tomorrow, the journey continues.

Alverca do Ribatejo to Vila Franca de Xira

The Central Route of the Camino Portugués offers a balance of charming countryside, local culture, and smaller towns that immerse you in the authentic rhythm of Portuguese life. As you move from Alverca do Ribatejo to Vila Franca de Xira, you'll notice the shifting scenery—from bustling streets to quiet rural pathways, and from industrial areas to serene riverside views. This section may not have the dramatic landscapes found later in Galicia, but it offers a glimpse into the real Portugal, often missed by tourists.

Leaving the suburban edges of Lisbon behind, the path from Alverca do Ribatejo leads you into the countryside, following roads and riverside trails. This stage covers roughly 10-12 kilometers (depending on your starting point), making it a manageable half-day walk for most pilgrims. Though the terrain is mostly flat, the day will take you through some urban sections before giving way to more scenic landscapes along the Tagus River.

There's something satisfying about watching the city slowly fade into the distance, with the river by your side and the distant hills beckoning you forward. As you approach Vila Franca de Xira, the scenery becomes more agricultural, and you'll start seeing the horses and bulls for which the region is known.

Alverca do Ribatejo

Alverca do Ribatejo is an industrial town, not particularly known for its beauty, but it serves as a practical starting point for pilgrims departing from Lisbon. Before you leave, you can explore the Museu do Ar (the Air Museum), dedicated to Portugal's aviation history. It's a unique stop if you have an interest in the subject, but most pilgrims will find themselves eager to hit the road.

If you need to fuel up before beginning your walk, Café Pastelaria Primavera offers excellent coffee and pastries that will keep you going until lunch. The café is a simple, no-frills stop, but that's part of its charm—it's a real slice of local life, away from the usual tourist spots.

The Walk: What to Expect

The initial stretch from Alverca can be a bit underwhelming, with roads and industrial buildings dotting the landscape. But soon, you'll find yourself walking alongside the Tagus River, and the air feels fresher, the walk more serene. The river will guide your way for much of the stage, offering a peaceful contrast to the earlier sections. Keep an eye out for local wildlife, particularly birds that frequent the riverbanks.

Along the way, you might pass through Sobralinho, a small area with little more than a few houses and local shops. It's a good spot for a brief rest if you need to stretch or grab a drink.

Vila Franca de Xira: The Destination

As you approach Vila Franca de Xira, the town's connection to horses and bulls becomes more apparent. Vila Franca is famous for its bullfighting tradition, which dates back centuries. While the tradition might not appeal to everyone, it is an integral part of local culture, and you'll likely see references to it as you wander through town.

The town itself is lively, with a riverside promenade that's perfect for a gentle stroll after your day's walk. You can also take in views of the Tagus River or relax in one of the local parks.

Where to Stay in Vila Franca de Xira

Vila Franca de Xira is relatively small, but it offers some comfortable accommodations for pilgrims looking to rest for the night.

- **Lezíria Parque Hotel**: A short distance from the town center, this hotel provides a cozy place to rest with clean rooms and friendly staff. It's modern but affordable, offering everything a weary pilgrim might need, including air conditioning and a hearty breakfast to fuel the next day's journey.

- **Hostel DP**: If you're looking for a more budget-friendly option, Hostel DP is a good alternative. It's located close to the train station and offers a shared kitchen, which can be handy for pilgrims who prefer preparing their own meals.

Where to Eat in Vila Franca de Xira

After a long day of walking, finding a good meal is key to recharging your body and spirit. Fortunately, Vila Franca de Xira has some excellent local dining spots that serve hearty, authentic Portuguese food.

- **Adega Ribatejana**: This charming restaurant offers traditional Portuguese cuisine, with an emphasis on grilled meats and fresh fish. Their portions are generous, and the atmosphere is welcoming, making it a popular spot for both locals and pilgrims. Try their bacalhau à brás (a traditional salted cod dish) or the famous Alheira sausage.

- **O Fuso**: Another great option, O Fuso specializes in regional dishes. Their menu is seasonal, with ingredients sourced locally, giving you an authentic taste of Ribatejo. The prices are reasonable, and the staff are happy to explain the menu to anyone unfamiliar with the dishes. A perfect spot to unwind with a glass of local wine.

Points of Interest

Though many pilgrims head straight to their albergue or hotel after arriving in Vila Franca de Xira, if you have the energy, there are a few local sights worth checking out:

- **Praça de Toiros Palha Blanco**: The town's bullring, Praça de Toiros Palha Blanco, is central to its bullfighting tradition. While not everyone will be interested in this part of Portuguese culture, the architecture is notable, and there's often a lot of activity around the bullring, especially during festivals.

- **Museu do Neo-Realismo**: If you're looking for something a bit different, this museum offers a glimpse into Portuguese neo-realism art and literature, focusing on social struggles and rural life in Portugal. It's an interesting contrast to the religious and historical themes you'll encounter along the Camino.

As your day in Vila Franca de Xira comes to a close, take a moment to reflect on the journey so far. This is still the early part of the Camino, but every step brings you closer to Santiago. Each town, with its distinct character and people, adds a unique chapter to your pilgrimage story.

From here, the Camino will begin to shift again, moving away from the flat riverside paths and into the rolling hills of central Portugal. But for now, enjoy the hospitality of Vila Franca de Xira and rest well—you'll need your strength for what lies ahead.

Vila Franca de Xira to Azambuja

The stretch from Vila Franca de Xira to Azambuja is a journey through the heart of rural Portugal, where the pace of life slows down, and the landscape opens into wide plains, agricultural fields, and riverbanks. This 18-kilometer segment of the Camino Portugués Central Route may not be the most challenging in terms of elevation, but it offers a chance to experience authentic, everyday Portuguese life away from the bustling cities. Along the way, you'll encounter small towns, open fields, and the ever-present companionship of the Tagus River on your left.

This is a tranquil stage, perfect for quiet reflection as you settle into the rhythm of the Camino. While it may not offer the dramatic scenery of later stages, it's a time to enjoy the peaceful countryside, and as you approach Azambuja, the landscape transforms into something distinctly rural, with fields and farms stretching out as far as the eye can see.

What to Expect on the Route

Leaving Vila Franca de Xira, the path leads you through a mix of agricultural land and quiet villages. The trail is mostly flat, and it can feel long at times, but the simplicity of the journey has its own charm. The wide, open spaces allow your mind to wander, and the presence of the river provides a sense of continuity and calm.

It's important to note that this stage doesn't offer many opportunities for shade, especially during the warmer months, so be sure to wear a hat and carry plenty of water. You won't encounter many shops or cafés along the way, so consider packing a snack to keep your energy up until you reach Azambuja.

Arrival in Azambuja

As you approach Azambuja, a small but welcoming town, the Camino leads you past fields of corn and vegetables, where farmers work diligently in the sun. The town itself is compact and easy to navigate, with a few quiet streets lined with local shops, cafés, and small businesses. The slower pace of life here will likely feel like a contrast to the bustling energy of earlier stops, but it's a welcome break before heading further north on your pilgrimage.

Azambuja may not be a tourist hotspot, but it offers all the essentials for a pilgrim to rest, eat, and rejuvenate for the next day's journey.

Hotel Recommendations

While Azambuja is a small town, it has several accommodations that cater to pilgrims, each offering simple yet comfortable options for an overnight stay.

- **Residencial Flor da Primavera**: This small guesthouse is known for its friendly service and clean rooms. It's located in the heart of Azambuja, just a short walk from the Camino trail. The rooms are basic but comfortable, with private bathrooms, making it a perfect resting spot for tired pilgrims. The staff are familiar with the needs of those walking the Camino and often go out of their way to offer assistance and advice.

- **Estalagem Vale Manso**: If you're looking for something a bit more luxurious (and don't mind a short taxi ride from the town center), Estalagem Vale Manso offers a charming rural retreat with a swimming pool and beautiful views of the surrounding countryside. Though it's not directly on the Camino, it provides a peaceful and relaxing environment to unwind after a long day of walking.

Restaurant Recommendations

For dining, Azambuja's restaurants focus on hearty, traditional Portuguese cuisine, with meals that will keep you full and energized for the next day's walk.

- **Restaurante A Praça**: Located right in the center of town, A Praça is a local favorite for its generous portions of grilled meats and fresh seafood. The atmosphere is cozy and welcoming, perfect for sitting down with fellow pilgrims to share stories over a filling meal. Their bacalhau (salt cod) dishes are especially popular, and the prices are reasonable, making it a good option for budget-conscious travelers.

- **O Afonso**: This family-run restaurant is known for its homemade, traditional dishes and friendly service. It's a great place to experience authentic Portuguese cooking, with dishes like caldo verde (a traditional soup made with kale and potatoes) and leitão assado (roast suckling pig). The portions are hearty, and the prices are affordable, making it a solid choice for pilgrims looking to refuel.

- **Café Central**: For something lighter, Café Central offers quick bites, sandwiches, and pastries. It's a great spot to grab a coffee and a snack if you want something simple and fast. The outdoor seating area makes it a pleasant stop for people-watching in the town's central square.

Tips for First-Time Pilgrims on this Stage

1. Prepare for the Sun: This stretch of the Camino can feel quite exposed, especially during the summer months. Be sure to carry a hat, sunscreen, and plenty of water, as there are few opportunities for shade along the way.

2. Bring Snacks: While Vila Franca de Xira has plenty of places to stock up, there are limited options for food along this particular route. Packing a snack, like fruit or nuts, will keep your energy levels steady until you reach Azambuja.

3. Pace Yourself: Though the terrain is flat and straightforward, the long, open stretches can be mentally challenging. Take breaks when you need to, and remember that there's no rush—enjoy the simplicity of walking through Portugal's countryside.

4. Embrace the Quiet: This stage is quieter than others, and you may not encounter as many fellow pilgrims. While some may find this solitude daunting, it's an opportunity to reflect and fully immerse yourself in the journey.

This stage of the Camino Portugués is less about the picturesque landmarks and more about embracing the rhythm of the pilgrimage. The rural beauty, the expansive fields, and the occasional glimpse of the river remind you of the simple joys of walking. It's a time to slow down, reconnect with yourself, and appreciate the quiet.

By the time you arrive in Azambuja, you'll feel the subtle shift from the more populated areas near Lisbon to the peaceful countryside that characterizes much of the Central Route. It's a gradual, grounding experience that prepares you for the challenges and rewards of the days ahead.

Though this stage may not be the most visually striking, it offers its own rewards—an opportunity to truly step into the pilgrim mindset, leaving behind the noise and distractions of everyday life as you continue your journey toward Santiago.

Azambuja to Santarém

The stretch from Azambuja to Santarém is an intriguing part of the Central Route of the Camino Portugués. It offers a gradual transition from the bustling energy of the Lisbon metropolitan area into the more rural, agricultural heart of Portugal. This stage is about 32 kilometers (20 miles) long, and it takes you through flat farmland, along the wide Tagus River, and past small, quiet villages.

While it's one of the longer stages of the Camino, the terrain is fairly flat, making it manageable for most pilgrims. As you walk through this stretch, you begin to experience a deeper connection to the land, especially with the sprawling vineyards and farms that define the landscape.

Leaving Azambuja

Azambuja is a small, quiet town located in the Ribatejo region. Known for its agricultural roots, this town feels like the perfect departure point as you head deeper into rural Portugal. If you stayed the night in Azambuja, you may have rested at Casa da Azambuja, a simple, comfortable lodging that provides pilgrims with the essentials: a clean bed, welcoming hosts, and a hearty meal to fuel your journey.

Before leaving Azambuja, grab breakfast at **Café Pinheiro,** where you can enjoy a strong coffee and fresh pastry to kickstart your day. The café is a popular stop for locals, giving you a chance to experience the rhythm of daily life in this small town.

The Journey Through Vineyards and Fields

As you set out from Azambuja, the path initially follows rural roads, gradually opening up to expansive fields and vineyards. This region is known for its winemaking, so the vineyards you pass aren't just for show—Portugal's Ribatejo wines are grown here. You might even notice the smell of the earth, rich and fertile, a reminder of the agricultural importance of this region.

While there aren't many villages between Azambuja and Santarém, you'll find plenty of opportunities to pause and take in the scenery. The walk can feel long at times, and on a hot day, the lack of shade can be challenging, but with a steady pace and breaks along the way, the journey is rewarding.

The trail often runs alongside the Tagus River, offering serene views of the water. This section is peaceful, with little traffic and only the occasional farmhouse dotting the horizon. It's a perfect time to let your mind wander, perhaps reflecting on your journey so far, or simply enjoying the present moment.

Arriving in Santarém

As you approach Santarém, you'll notice the landscape beginning to shift. The terrain becomes hillier, and soon enough, you'll see the city itself, perched atop a hill overlooking the surrounding plains. This ancient city, once a Roman settlement, is steeped in history and offers a striking contrast to the flat lands you've been walking through.

The final stretch involves a bit of an uphill climb into Santarém, but once you reach the top, the reward is well worth the effort. The city is known for its Gothic architecture and historical significance, making it a fascinating place to explore.

Where to Stay in Santarém

Santarém offers a range of accommodations suitable for pilgrims looking for both comfort and a taste of local hospitality.

- **Hotel Umu**: This modern hotel is just a short walk from the city center. It offers comfortable rooms, and the staff is friendly and accommodating to pilgrims. After a long day of walking, the clean, spacious rooms and hot showers here can feel like pure luxury.

- **N1 Hostel Apartments and Suites**: For those seeking something more budget-friendly but still stylish, N1 Hostel offers a variety of options from dorm beds to private rooms. It's a social place with a common area where pilgrims often gather to share stories of their day's walk.

- **Casa do Alfageme**: Located in a historical building with rustic charm, this cozy guesthouse offers a more intimate stay. The warm ambiance and home-cooked meals make it feel like you've been welcomed into a local's home.

Dining in Santarém

After a long day on the trail, food becomes a central focus for most pilgrims. Santarém does not disappoint, offering a range of traditional Portuguese dishes that will satisfy any hunger.

- **Taberna do Quinzena**: One of the most beloved restaurants in Santarém, this is the place to go if you want to try hearty, traditional Portuguese cuisine. Their Cozido à Portuguesa (Portuguese stew) is a local favorite, and the portions are generous. The restaurant has been around for decades, with an old-world charm that adds to the experience.

- **O Manel**: A family-run restaurant located in the heart of the city, O Manel serves fresh, locally sourced meals. Their bacalhau com natas (codfish with cream) is a must-try, and they offer a pilgrim menu that provides great value for the money.

- **Pastelaria Bijou**: If you have a sweet tooth, this pastry shop is a great spot to try local desserts. Grab a pastel de nata (custard tart) or a bolo de arroz (rice cake) and a coffee as an afternoon treat while wandering through Santarém's historic streets.

Exploring Santarém

Once you've settled into your accommodations and satisfied your appetite, take some time to explore Santarém. The city is often called the "Capital of the Gothic" for its stunning collection of medieval buildings. The Igreja de São João de Alporão, a 12th-century church, and the Igreja da Graça are both remarkable examples of Gothic architecture and worth a visit.

For panoramic views of the countryside, head to the Portas do Sol gardens, where you can take in sweeping vistas of the Tagus River and the fertile plains that stretch out below. This peaceful park is a perfect spot to reflect on your journey, with benches and shady spots where you can rest your legs and enjoy the serenity of the surroundings.

The stage from Azambuja to Santarém may not have the dramatic landscapes of later stages, but its quiet beauty lies in its simplicity. Walking through vineyards, farmlands, and alongside the Tagus River, this section of the Camino gives you a sense of the agricultural roots that define much of Portugal.

Arriving in Santarém, with its rich history and Gothic architecture, feels like a reward for your efforts. Whether you spend the evening strolling through the streets or enjoying a hearty meal at a local restaurant, the city offers a perfect mix of rest and cultural discovery.

For first-time pilgrims, this stage is a gentle introduction to the longer days ahead and a reminder that the Camino is as much about the small moments—the quiet stretches of road, the unexpected conversation with a fellow pilgrim—as it is about reaching Santiago.

Santarém to Golegã

The stretch from Santarém to Golegã is a beautiful, tranquil part of the Camino Portugués. As you leave the fortified hilltop town of Santarém, known for its stunning views over the Tagus River, the path winds through agricultural fields, vineyards, and quiet rural villages. It's a stage that brings a sense of serenity, with wide open spaces and a chance to reflect on the journey so far.

This part of the Camino offers a shift in scenery as you move away from the rolling hills and begin to see more of Portugal's fertile farmland. The landscapes here are vast and open, with the simplicity of rural life unfolding around you—fields of corn, tomato, and olive groves stretch for miles. It's a slower, quieter section of the Camino, and by the time you reach Golegã, the "Capital of the Horse," you'll feel a deep connection to Portugal's rustic heart.

Leaving Santarém

Santarém, with its medieval streets and significant history, is a town that begs for exploration. Before setting off, many pilgrims take the time to visit the Igreja da Graça, with its Gothic architecture, or stroll along the Porta do Sol, a garden that offers sweeping views of the Tagus River and the plains beyond. The departure from Santarém marks the beginning of a more peaceful section of the Camino, where the towns become smaller, and the rhythm of rural life becomes more apparent.

Make sure to fill your water bottle before leaving Santarém, as services are limited on the way to Golegã.

The Route: Fields, Farms, and Solitude

The path from Santarém to Golegã covers about 30 kilometers, depending on the exact route you follow. The terrain is mostly flat, making for an easier walking day compared to some of the earlier stages. As you make your way out of Santarém, you'll cross through fields and farmland, often sharing the path with tractors and the occasional farmer going about their daily routine. The air is fresh, and the landscape feels expansive.

This is a quieter stretch, and you may find yourself walking alone for long periods, though the solitude often brings a welcome sense of peace. The few villages you'll pass through are small, with limited services, so it's wise to carry snacks and enough water for the day. This is the kind of stage that allows you to fully immerse yourself in the natural surroundings, with the rolling fields offering an almost meditative experience.

Arriving in Golegã: The Horse Capital

As you approach Golegã, the landscape begins to change. The town is known as the "Capital of the Horse" due to its rich equestrian traditions, and it hosts the National Horse Fair every November. Even if you're not visiting during the fair, Golegã has a deep connection to Lusitano horses, and you may see them being ridden or trained as you walk into town. The town itself is charming, with cobbled streets and whitewashed buildings that give it a distinctively Portuguese feel.

Where to Stay in Golegã

While Golegã is small, it offers some lovely accommodations for weary pilgrims. Whether you're looking for a simple albergue or a more comfortable stay, you'll find options that cater to different preferences.

- **Casa dos Ofícios**: A cozy guesthouse with a warm, welcoming atmosphere, Casa dos Ofícios is popular among pilgrims. The rooms are tastefully decorated, and the communal spaces invite relaxation after a long day of walking. It's a great place to rest and connect with other travelers.

- **Quinta dos Álamos**: For those looking to experience a bit of the equestrian culture that Golegã is famous for, Quinta dos Álamos is a beautiful farm stay where you can unwind in the heart of horse country. The rooms are charming, and there's plenty of outdoor space to relax and soak in the peaceful atmosphere.

- **Albergue de Peregrinos de São Caetano**: This simple albergue offers all the basics that a pilgrim needs—clean beds, hot showers, and a friendly environment. It's a budget-friendly option that keeps you close to the Camino experience.

Where to Eat in Golegã

After a long day on the road, Golegã offers several dining spots that serve hearty Portuguese meals to refuel your energy.

- **Restaurante O Lusitano**: True to Golegã's equestrian heritage, this restaurant embraces the local horse culture in its decor and atmosphere. The menu is full of traditional Portuguese dishes like bacalhau (salted cod) and cozido à portuguesa (a rich stew). The portions are generous, and the food is prepared with local ingredients.

- **Adega Ribatejana**: A family-run restaurant that serves classic Portuguese fare, Adega Ribatejana is known for its welcoming service and homemade flavors. Try the feijoada (a hearty bean and meat stew) or the grilled meats, which are local favorites.

- **Cafe Central**: A more casual option, Café Central is a great spot to relax with a coffee or a light meal. The café's location in the town center makes it a convenient place to stop for a break or a quick bite.

What to Expect Along the Way

As with most sections of the Camino, the journey from Santarém to Golegã is not just about the destination. The walk itself is the highlight—long stretches of road where you can lose yourself in thought, appreciate the natural beauty around you, or simply focus on putting one foot in front of the other.

While there aren't many villages or services on this stage, you'll likely encounter a few local farmers tending their fields or passing tractors kicking up dust in the distance. The openness of the land can feel refreshing after walking through more populated areas earlier on the Camino.

A Day to Reflect

The Santarém to Golegã stage is a time for reflection. The quiet surroundings and long stretches of farmland offer the perfect backdrop for thinking about the journey you've undertaken so far. This is a stage where many pilgrims find a sense of peace, away from the distractions of towns and cities. By the time you reach Golegã, you'll be ready to rest and recharge, knowing that the Camino still has more to offer in the days ahead.

This stage might feel long and quiet, but it's a reminder of the simplicity that makes the Camino so powerful. It's not just about reaching the end, but about the steps in between—each one bringing you closer to Santiago, and to yourself.

Golegã to Tomar

This stage of the Camino Portugués from Golegã to Tomar feels like a journey through time and nature. As you leave behind the quiet horse town of Golegã, you step into a world that mixes medieval history with peaceful farmlands and vineyards. This stretch offers a perfect balance between pastoral beauty and rich cultural heritage, leading you toward Tomar, one of the most historically significant towns on the Camino.

The distance between Golegã and Tomar is about 30 km. While not an easy stroll, it's manageable with the right pace and mindset. The terrain is a mix of rural roads, fields, and some paved paths, which can be demanding after several days of walking, especially in warmer weather. You'll pass through small villages and open stretches, giving you a variety of landscapes to enjoy and reflect upon as you move forward.

Highlights Along the Way

- **Quinta Cardiga**: About halfway between Golegã and Tomar, you'll pass by the old estate of Quinta da Cardiga, an elegant 16th-century manor once owned by the Knights Templar. The faded beauty of this estate gives you a sense of history, and while it's not open to the public, the exterior is well worth a pause.

- **Olive Groves and Vineyards**: This section of the Camino is rich with agricultural landscapes, especially olive trees and vineyards. Walking through these open fields, with the smell of the earth and the sight of ancient trees, brings a calmness that's hard to find elsewhere.

Arriving in Tomar

Arriving in Tomar feels like a fitting reward after the day's walk. Known for its connection to the Knights Templar, Tomar is a charming and compact town, perfect for wandering its narrow streets or sitting in a plaza with a cold drink. You'll immediately notice the Convent of Christ, a UNESCO World Heritage site, towering over the town—a must-see for anyone passing through.

Hotel Recommendations

After a long day's walk, finding a comfortable place to rest in Tomar is essential. Here are a few options that cater to pilgrims and first-time visitors alike:

- **Hotel dos Templários**: Located near the river in the heart of Tomar, this four-star hotel is known for its spacious rooms, beautiful garden, and pool—an absolute luxury after a day of walking. It's also reasonably priced given its high standards, making it a popular choice among pilgrims looking to indulge a little.

- **Hostel 2300 Thomar**: If you're looking for something a bit more budget-friendly but still cozy, this hostel is a fantastic option. It's modern, colorful, and offers both private rooms and dormitory-style beds. The communal atmosphere makes it easy to meet fellow pilgrims.

- **Flattered to be in Tomar**: For those seeking something more unique, these boutique apartments offer a homely feel with chic design. It's ideal for pilgrims who want more privacy and the ability to cook their own meals.

Restaurant Recommendations

Tomar offers a variety of dining options, from traditional Portuguese cuisine to lighter fare for weary pilgrims:

- **Taverna Antiqua**: Located in the historic center, this medieval-themed tavern offers an immersive experience along with hearty meals. The menu focuses on traditional Portuguese dishes, such as roasted meats, stews, and fresh bread. The ambiance is warm and perfect for enjoying a meal after a long day.

- **Restaurante Sabores ao Rubro**: A great option for those wanting a more modern twist on Portuguese cuisine. This restaurant prides itself on using local ingredients with a contemporary flair. Whether you're in the mood for seafood, meat, or a vegetarian option, Sabores ao Rubro provides a comforting, flavorful experience.

- **O Tabuleiro**: Popular among pilgrims and locals alike, this small restaurant serves authentic Portuguese home-cooked meals. Their portion sizes are generous, and the staff is welcoming, offering dishes like codfish with potatoes, grilled meats, and hearty soups.

What to Do in Tomar

After resting and refueling, Tomar invites you to dive into its rich history and stunning architecture. Take time to explore:

- **The Convent of Christ**: This former stronghold of the Knights Templar is an absolute highlight. With its mix of

Gothic, Manueline, and Renaissance styles, it's one of Portugal's most impressive historical monuments. Be sure to visit the Charola, the rotunda that was the Templar's private oratory, and wander through the convent's cloisters.

- **Tomar Castle**: Situated next to the Convent of Christ, the castle offers panoramic views of the town and the surrounding countryside. The walk up to the castle is steep but rewarding, especially for the sense of history and the peaceful atmosphere at the top.

- **Aqueduct of Pegões**: Just outside Tomar, this impressive aqueduct is a feat of 17th-century engineering. If your feet are still willing, it's worth the walk to admire the scale of this structure up close.

Walking from Golegã to Tomar is not just a physical journey; it's a pilgrimage through history, nature, and self-reflection. The quiet roads, the vineyards, and the sight of the Convent of Christ looming in the distance all weave together into an experience that's both humbling and uplifting. By the time you reach Tomar, you'll likely find yourself reflecting not only on the history of the place but also on the distance you've traveled—both in kilometers and within yourself.

This stage offers pilgrims a unique mix of rural beauty and cultural richness, making it one of the most memorable parts of the Camino Portugués. Whether you find yourself resting in the shade of an olive tree or standing in awe at the gates of the Convent of Christ, this stretch from Golegã to Tomar will stay with you long after you've left it behind.

Tomar to Alvaiázere

The route from Tomar to Alvaiázere is a captivating stage of the Camino Portugués, offering a blend of quiet rural life, hilly landscapes, and small, welcoming villages. After soaking in the historical splendor of Tomar, this next stretch shifts your focus toward the simplicity of the Portuguese countryside. It's a day that balances challenge and beauty, with hills beginning to play a more noticeable role in the terrain, all while offering moments of peace and reflection on the Camino.

This section spans about 32 km, and although the distance might seem daunting, the landscapes help soothe the journey. The terrain is a mix of small rural roads, forest paths, and agricultural land, with some steady inclines as you begin to leave the flatlands behind and enter more hilly regions. As you move closer to Alvaiázere, the Camino becomes quieter and more intimate, with fewer pilgrims on the path and more chances to enjoy the solitude of the natural surroundings.

Highlights Along the Way

- **Valinhos Forest**: As you leave Tomar, the first few kilometers take you through the peaceful Valinhos Forest. Walking under the shade of eucalyptus and pine trees provides some relief from the sun and allows for a peaceful start to the day.

- **Rural Villages**: The Camino passes through several small, traditional villages, such as Casais and Cabaços, where you'll find local cafes to grab a quick bite or refresh with a cold drink. These villages give you a glimpse into the quiet, agricultural life that has remained unchanged for centuries.

- **Views of Serra de Alvaiázere**: As you approach Alvaiázere, the Serra de Alvaiázere hills rise in the distance, marking the shift from the flatter landscapes of earlier stages to a more rolling, rugged terrain. This change in scenery offers a refreshing challenge and beautiful vistas that will stay with you long after your Camino is over.

Arriving in Alvaiázere

Alvaiázere is a small but charming town, offering a much-needed rest after a long day of walking. Though it's not as well-known as some of the larger stops along the Camino, its quiet streets and friendly locals make it a pleasant place to pause. The town is nestled in a valley surrounded by hills, giving it a serene and rural feel that contrasts with the larger, more bustling towns further back on the route.

Hotel Recommendations

Alvaiázere may not have a wide array of accommodation options, but what it lacks in quantity, it makes up for in warmth and hospitality:

- **O Alvaiazere**: This small but cozy guesthouse offers clean, comfortable rooms and a welcoming atmosphere. Located centrally in the town, it's a convenient place to rest after a long day. The owner is known for going above and beyond to make pilgrims feel at home, offering a home-cooked breakfast and even helping with laundry.

- **Casa da Rosa**: Situated a bit outside the main town, this rural guesthouse provides a more peaceful setting, surrounded by nature. If you're looking for a quiet night's rest in a more private, picturesque environment, Casa da Rosa offers that retreat. The rooms are spacious and the hosts offer excellent hospitality, including meals made from local produce.

Restaurant Recommendations

Alvaiázere's food scene reflects its rural roots, with simple, hearty meals that nourish body and soul. Here are a couple of recommended spots:

- **Restaurante Churrasqueira O Fidalgo**: This small, unassuming restaurant serves up generous portions of traditional Portuguese dishes, especially grilled meats like pork and chicken. It's a no-frills place, but after a long day of walking, the hearty meals hit the spot. The local red wine is a perfect accompaniment to the food, and the friendly service adds to the experience.

- **Café Restaurante O Afonso**: Another great spot for pilgrims, this café offers simple yet flavorful meals. From grilled fish to stews and rice dishes, the food here feels like a taste of home. The outdoor seating is perfect for relaxing in the evening, watching the town go by as you recharge.

What to Do in Alvaiázere

Alvaiázere itself is a quiet town, with fewer large-scale attractions compared to other stops, but it does offer some interesting spots for pilgrims wanting to explore:

- **Serra de Alvaiázere**: For those with the energy, a short detour from the town leads to the nearby hills. If you're up for it, a walk up these hills offers spectacular views over the surrounding countryside. It's a great way to reflect on your journey while surrounded by nature.

- **Local Churches**: Alvaiázere is home to several small, historic churches that are worth visiting for a quiet moment of reflection. The town's humble yet beautiful chapels provide peaceful places to rest and connect with the spiritual side of the Camino.

The stretch from Tomar to Alvaiázere is an important transition on the Camino Portugués. You leave behind the grand history of Tomar and step into a quieter, more rural world, where the Camino feels less about sightseeing and more about the journey itself. The rolling hills, the quiet roads, and the small villages all contribute to a sense of peaceful solitude, offering a perfect space for personal reflection.

By the time you arrive in Alvaiázere, your legs may be tired, but your spirit will be lighter. It's a day that reminds you that the Camino is as much about the quiet moments as it is about the grand ones. Each step brings you closer to Santiago, not only physically but mentally and emotionally.

Chapter 5

Stage 8 - 17

Alvaiázere to Ansião

This stretch of the Camino Portugués offers a tranquil yet invigorating journey through the heart of rural Portugal. As you leave the small town of Alvaiázere, you'll quickly find yourself surrounded by olive groves, eucalyptus trees, and serene farmlands. The Camino here feels personal and peaceful, making it a chance to reflect while immersing yourself in the natural landscape.

The distance from Alvaiázere to Ansião is about 15 km, making it a relatively short but rewarding stage. The terrain is gentle, with some rolling hills that give you a pleasant mix of challenge and ease. Shaded paths lined with trees offer relief on warm days, and the occasional small village breaks up the walk, offering rest stops and refreshments.

Highlights Along the Way

- **Eucalyptus Forests**: The scent of eucalyptus fills the air as you pass through these groves, adding a fresh, earthy fragrance to your walk. These forests are characteristic of this region and offer a serene, almost meditative experience.

- **Rural Villages**: As you walk through small villages, you'll get a glimpse into the slower, simpler way of life in this part of Portugal. Farmers tending to their fields, the quiet hum of village life, and friendly locals greet pilgrims with a smile or a wave.

Arriving in Ansião

Ansião is a small, unassuming town, but its charm lies in its authenticity. The town offers a quiet rest stop for pilgrims, with enough amenities to recharge after your walk. While not as historically significant as some other stops, it's a welcome break and gives you the opportunity to enjoy the rhythm of daily life in a rural Portuguese town.

Hotel Recommendations

- **Hotel O Cavalinho**: This hotel is a great option for pilgrims looking for a simple and comfortable place to stay. The rooms are clean, the staff is friendly, and the location is convenient for those passing through. It's not fancy, but it's perfect for a good night's rest.

- **Albergue O Ninho**: A more budget-friendly option, this albergue offers communal accommodation for pilgrims. It's simple but welcoming, with shared spaces that encourage conversation with other travelers.

Restaurant Recommendations

- **Restaurante O Ansião**: This local eatery serves up traditional Portuguese fare with hearty portions. It's a great place to enjoy regional dishes like bacalhau (salted cod) or cozido (a Portuguese stew). The cozy atmosphere makes it a favorite among pilgrims passing through.

- **Pastelaria Pôr do Sol**: If you're craving something sweet or a light snack, this café offers a selection of delicious pastries, coffee, and sandwiches. It's a good stop to fuel up before heading out for the next stage.

Ansião to Coimbra

The journey from Ansião to Coimbra takes you further into the heart of Portugal. This stage is longer, around 35 km, and while the distance might feel daunting, the route is full of rich landscapes and historical intrigue that keep you motivated. As you approach Coimbra, the landscape shifts from rural charm to the bustling energy of one of Portugal's most famous university cities.

The terrain from Ansião to Coimbra is varied, with a few hills and plenty of stretches through fields, forests, and small villages. You'll encounter both gravel paths and paved roads, with some sections that require careful navigation, especially on days when the weather is unpredictable. It's a longer stage, so pace yourself and take advantage of the scenic rest stops along the way.

Highlights Along the Way

- **Small Villages**: Like the earlier stages, this route takes you through several quaint villages. These offer a chance to experience Portugal's rural culture firsthand, with quiet streets, family-run farms, and traditional homes dotting the landscape.

- **Nature Reserves and Forests**: You'll pass through lush forests and nature reserves that create a peaceful environment for walking. The abundance of trees provides welcome shade, and the bird songs add a soundtrack to your journey.

Arriving in Coimbra

Coimbra is a world apart from the rural stages that precede it. Known for its prestigious university, Coimbra buzzes with youthful energy and historical depth. The town is perched on a hill above the River Mondego, and its steep streets lead to a maze of old buildings, lively squares, and ancient sites. The change in pace from the peaceful countryside to the vibrant city is both energizing and rewarding.

Hotel Recommendations

- **Tivoli Coimbra Hotel**: This modern four-star hotel offers a blend of comfort and convenience in the heart of the city. Spacious rooms, excellent service, and proximity to Coimbra's major attractions make it a great choice for pilgrims who want a touch of luxury.

- **Hotel Astória**: For something more classic, the Hotel Astória is housed in a beautiful 1920s building with charming Art Deco interiors. Its central location makes it easy to explore the city, and the historical ambiance provides a wonderful contrast to the modern world outside.

- **Albergue de Peregrinos Rainha Santa Isabel**: A perfect option for those on a budget, this pilgrim's hostel offers clean, basic accommodations. It's a good place to connect with fellow pilgrims and share stories of the journey so far.

Restaurant Recommendations

- **Zé Manel dos Ossos**: This tiny, rustic restaurant is known for its authentic Portuguese dishes. It's a local institution, offering hearty meals such as feijoada (bean stew) and leitão (suckling pig). It's a bit of a hidden gem and fills up quickly, so be prepared to wait—but it's worth it!

- **Solar do Bacalhau**: Specializing in Portugal's national dish, bacalhau, this restaurant serves up endless variations of salted cod. Whether you like it grilled, baked, or stewed, you'll find something to satisfy your appetite here. The portions are generous, and the atmosphere is lively.

- **Pastelaria Briosa**: If you have a sweet tooth, don't miss this famous pastry shop. Their pastéis de nata (custard tarts) are some of the best in the region, and the variety of cakes and pastries on offer is sure to please any pilgrim looking for a sugary pick-me-up.

What to Do in Coimbra

While in Coimbra, take some time to explore the city's rich history:

- **University of Coimbra**: One of the oldest universities in Europe, this UNESCO World Heritage site is a must-visit. The Joanina Library is especially stunning, with its ornate baroque design and vast collection of ancient books.

- **Old Cathedral of Coimbra (Sé Velha)**: This Romanesque cathedral is an architectural gem, standing as a testament to the city's medieval past. Its fortress-like appearance makes it unique, and stepping inside offers a peaceful escape from the busy streets.

- **Monastery of Santa Clara-a-Velha**: Situated across the river, this gothic monastery is both haunting and beautiful. Its flooded ruins are a reminder of the city's complex history, and the nearby museum offers insight into the life of the nuns who once lived there.

Walking from Alvaiázere to Coimbra provides a shift from rural serenity to the excitement of an urban destination, giving you the best of both worlds on the Camino. The path is long, but the reward of reaching Coimbra—a city steeped in history, culture, and life—makes it a truly memorable stage. By the time you arrive, you'll have walked through fields and forests, past ancient olive trees, and into the heart of one of Portugal's most vibrant cities. It's a stage that reminds you of the diversity and depth of the Camino Portugués, making every step forward feel like progress not just on the map, but within yourself.

Coimbra to Mealhada

Leaving the historic charm of Coimbra behind, you'll embark on the next leg of the Camino Portugués toward Mealhada. This section is often peaceful, passing through small villages, vineyards, and patches of forests that invite quiet reflection. With around 22 km to cover, it's a relatively moderate stretch, but the sun and terrain can make it feel longer than expected. That said, the transition from Coimbra's urban energy to the rural landscape gives you space to think, unwind, and simply walk.

The walk from Coimbra to Mealhada offers a gentle mix of urban paths and rural landscapes. The terrain starts out fairly straightforward, with some roads leading out of Coimbra, and gradually gives way to more countryside, offering relief from the busier city atmosphere. Though mostly flat, the distance can feel taxing if the weather is hot, so taking regular breaks is wise. The rhythm of passing through quaint Portuguese villages gives this stretch a serene, timeless quality.

Arriving in Mealhada

Known for its famous Leitão à Bairrada (roast suckling pig), Mealhada may surprise you with its culinary reputation despite being a smaller town. Upon arrival, the smell of roasting pork often fills the air, tempting pilgrims to indulge in the local specialty. The town is welcoming, offering a good variety of accommodations and eateries for those in need of rest and sustenance.

Hotel Recommendations in Mealhada

- **Quinta dos Três Pinheiros**: Located just outside the center of Mealhada, this hotel offers spacious rooms and a relaxing atmosphere, surrounded by nature. The outdoor pool is perfect for cooling off after a long day's walk, and the onsite restaurant serves local dishes, including their famous roasted pork.

- **Residencial Hilário**: For those looking for a simpler, more budget-friendly option, this guesthouse offers comfortable rooms with a homely vibe. The owners are friendly, and it's conveniently located near restaurants and the main road for easy access to the next stage of the Camino.

- **Hotel Alegre**: A charming hotel nestled within the Luso mountains, just a short drive from Mealhada. It offers cozy rooms and beautiful views, making it an ideal retreat for weary pilgrims seeking peace and a touch of luxury. It's close to Termas de Luso, where you can relax in thermal baths—a treat for sore muscles.

Restaurant Recommendations in Mealhada

- **Restaurante Pedro dos Leitões**: If you're in Mealhada, trying the famed Leitão à Bairrada is almost a must. This iconic restaurant has been serving roast suckling pig for decades, and its popularity among locals and pilgrims alike speaks for itself. The crispy skin and tender meat are an experience on their own, paired perfectly with regional wine from Bairrada.

- **O Castiço**: Another great option if you're looking to taste the best of Mealhada's local cuisine. The menu offers traditional Portuguese dishes, and their suckling pig is just as delicious as any in town. They also serve hearty soups and grilled meats, making it a great spot to recharge.

Mealhada to Águeda

The next stage from Mealhada to Águeda is about 25 km and offers a blend of rural walking and a few steeper inclines. As you walk through forests of pine and eucalyptus, the freshness in the air gives you renewed energy, and the quiet paths offer a calm that feels miles away from the hustle of urban life. You'll pass through several small hamlets along the way, giving you a glimpse of rural Portuguese life at its most authentic.

This section has a little more variety in its terrain. While most of the path is flat and shaded, there are moments of climbing that can challenge tired legs. The surrounding countryside, with its vineyards and forests, offers much-needed shade, and there's a tranquility in the air that makes it easy to find a walking rhythm.

One of the highlights of this stage is walking through the pine forests, where the aromatic scent of pine and eucalyptus fills the air, making for a refreshing change from the sunbaked roads. Be prepared for a couple of steeper sections, particularly as you approach Águeda, but nothing too overwhelming.

Arriving in Águeda

Águeda is a vibrant town, often known for its colorful umbrella installation that decorates the streets during the summer months. It's a town full of energy, offering pilgrims a warm welcome after a day's trek. The mix of traditional charm and modern creativity makes it a delightful stop on the Camino.

Hotel Recommendations in Águeda

- **In Gold Hotel & Spa**: A contemporary hotel located on the outskirts of Águeda, this spot is great for pilgrims seeking comfort and a touch of luxury. Its modern design, spacious rooms, and excellent breakfast offerings make it a perfect place to rest. If your feet need some serious recovery, the spa facilities provide a little extra comfort.

- **Residencial Celeste**: A more budget-friendly option that offers clean, simple rooms and excellent hospitality. It's conveniently located near the center of town, so it's easy to explore Águeda after you've settled in. The owners are known for their warmth and helpfulness, making this a popular choice among pilgrims.

- **Hotel Conde de Águeda**: A charming boutique hotel right in the heart of the town. The rooftop terrace offers stunning views of the town and the surrounding countryside, especially at sunset. It's a lovely place to unwind with a drink after a long day's walk.

Restaurant Recommendations in Águeda

- **O Bairro**: This lively restaurant offers a mix of Portuguese and international dishes, with generous portions that will satisfy even the hungriest pilgrims. Their grilled meats and seafood are particularly popular, and the atmosphere is warm and welcoming, perfect for a post-walk meal.

- **Restaurante D. Afonso**: For those who want to try traditional Portuguese food in a homely setting, this is a great option. Their bacalhau (salted cod) dishes are a hit, and the menu offers a range of hearty, comforting meals. The service is attentive, and the prices are reasonable, making it ideal for pilgrims looking for a relaxed dining experience.

The stretch from Coimbra to Águeda is one of contrasts. You begin in a historic university town filled with life and end in the artistic, modern town of Águeda, passing through rural landscapes and quiet villages along the way. The journey is at once physically demanding and mentally relaxing, as the paths through forests and farmlands give your mind space to wander, while the occasional climb keeps you focused on the task at hand.

Each stop offers its own charm—Mealhada with its famous roast pork and Águeda with its artistic flair—giving pilgrims a taste of both Portugal's culinary traditions and its creative spirit. Walking these paths, you get the sense that the Camino is as much about the journey as it is about the destination, with each town offering new experiences to reflect on and enjoy.

Água to Albergaria-a-Velha

Leaving Água behind, you'll find yourself walking through quiet forests, charming villages, and open farmland. This 16 km stretch between Água and Albergaria-a-Velha is not overly demanding, but it still offers plenty of picturesque moments that will leave an impression on you.

The path from Água to Albergaria-a-Velha is gentle, with a relatively even terrain compared to other sections of the Camino. As you walk, the trail alternates between dirt tracks through forests, rural roads, and a few paved sections, providing a nice balance of different terrains. The forests offer shade, and the farmland opens up views of rolling hills, giving you moments of serenity along the way.

Highlights Along the Way

- **Small Villages**: This section passes through quaint, sleepy villages, such as Mourisca do Vouga and Serém de Baixo, where time seems to slow down. Pilgrims often find these spots ideal for short breaks, enjoying a coffee at a local café or simply taking in the atmosphere of rural life.

- **Forested Paths**: The natural beauty along this route is undeniable, with forested sections offering peace and tranquility. These wooded trails are often described as a soothing contrast to the more open stretches of farmland that follow.

Arriving in Albergaria-a-Velha

Albergaria-a-Velha, a small but vibrant town, provides a restful stop for pilgrims after a peaceful walk. Though small in size, it has all the essentials to rest, refuel, and prepare for the next stage of the journey. Its friendly atmosphere makes pilgrims feel welcome and at ease.

Hotel Recommendations

- **Hotel Solar das Laranjeiras:** This cozy, family-run hotel is perfect for those looking for a quiet place to rest. Its peaceful garden and simple, comfortable rooms offer the kind of respite a pilgrim needs after a day on the road. Located just a short walk from the main town center, it's both convenient and charming.

- **Albergue Rainha D. Teresa**: For those traveling on a budget, this albergue offers a friendly and communal atmosphere. The dormitory-style rooms are clean, and it's a popular stop among pilgrims, making it an excellent place to share stories and connect with fellow travelers.

Restaurant Recommendations

- **Restaurante Solar dos Presuntos**: A local favorite, this family-run restaurant serves traditional Portuguese fare with generous portions. After a long day's walk, the hearty dishes—like grilled meats and codfish—will feel like the perfect reward.

- **O Borges**: A small, no-fuss café that serves simple, flavorful meals. Popular among both locals and pilgrims, it's an ideal spot for a quick bite or a quiet evening meal.

Albergaria-a-Velha to São João da Madeira

This next stage of the Camino, covering about 29 km, takes you from Albergaria-a-Velha to São João da Madeira. While slightly longer and more physically demanding than the previous day's walk, this section carries you through a blend of rural roads and the occasional bustling village, offering a taste of both quiet and vibrant Portugal.

The terrain is relatively mixed, with some gentle climbs as you approach São João da Madeira. The day starts off with tranquil countryside, but as you near your destination, you'll encounter more urban areas, signaling the approach of São João da Madeira. It's a long day, so taking breaks in the small villages along the way is highly recommended.

Highlights Along the Way

- **Branca**: About halfway through the day's walk, you'll pass through Branca, a small village that makes for a great spot to stop, rest, and grab a snack. It's a sleepy village but a comforting stop before the final stretch into São João da Madeira.

- **Forested Hills and Farmland**: The route includes a few sections where you'll walk through lush forests and farmland. The rolling hills provide a beautiful backdrop, especially when bathed in the warm afternoon light.

Arriving in São João da Madeira

Known for its industrial roots, particularly in the hat-making industry, São João da Madeira is an energetic town with a strong local character. While not as historically significant as some of the previous stops, it offers plenty of modern conveniences for pilgrims.

Hotel Recommendations

- **Hotel Golden Tulip**: A comfortable and modern option, this four-star hotel is a great choice for those wanting to indulge in a bit of luxury after a long day of walking. The rooms are spacious, and the staff is attentive. It's located close to the town center, making it convenient for exploring.

- **AS São João da Madeira:** If you're looking for something more budget-friendly, this hotel is a clean and practical option. The rooms are simple but comfortable, offering everything you need for a restful night.

- **Albergue de Peregrinos São João da Madeira**: Pilgrims on a budget will appreciate the simplicity and warmth of this albergue. The dormitory setup encourages a communal experience, making it easy to connect with other pilgrims.

Restaurant Recommendations

- **Casa da Criatividade:** A cozy restaurant known for its creative approach to traditional Portuguese cuisine. The menu changes frequently, but everything is freshly made and beautifully presented. It's a bit of an upscale option, ideal if you're looking to celebrate reaching São João da Madeira.

- **Restaurante Ferrinho:** For a more laid-back dining experience, Ferrinho is a local favorite. The atmosphere is warm, and the dishes are comforting—think grilled meats, hearty stews, and fresh seafood. It's a place where pilgrims can sit back, enjoy a filling meal, and relax after a long day.

The transition from Águeda to São João da Madeira provides pilgrims with a satisfying blend of rural tranquility and urban energy. The forests and farmlands offer moments of peaceful reflection, while the towns of Albergaria-a-Velha and São João da Madeira provide the comforts of modernity. This section of the Camino Portugués reminds you that every day brings its own rewards, whether it's the view of rolling hills or a warm plate of traditional Portuguese food at the end of a long journey.

Each step you take on this route brings you closer not just to Santiago but to a deeper understanding of Portugal's landscapes, culture, and your own pilgrimage.

São João da Madeira to Porto

As you journey from São João da Madeira toward Porto, you'll feel the landscape gradually shift, moving from quiet villages and industrial areas into the energy of one of Portugal's most vibrant cities. This stage, spanning roughly 27 km, is a mix of rural charm and urban sprawl. Though the walk isn't too demanding in terms of elevation, the distance can feel long after consecutive days on the Camino, so pacing yourself is key.

The Path to Porto

Leaving São João da Madeira, the first part of your journey will take you through a mixture of paved roads and suburban areas. The region is known for its industry, but there are still pockets of green and the occasional charming village to pass through. The further you go, the more you'll notice the landscape becoming busier, with signs of Porto's outskirts appearing.

While there might not be many jaw-dropping views or monuments along this stretch, the excitement builds as you approach Porto, one of the Camino's highlights.

Arriving in Porto

Porto, with its cobblestone streets, river views, and iconic tiled buildings, is an essential stop on the Camino Portugués. As soon as you cross into the city, you'll be welcomed by the unmistakable charm of its bustling streets and historic landmarks. It's a city that merges old-world charm with modern flair, making it the perfect place to rest and explore before continuing north.

Hotel Recommendations in Porto

Porto offers a wide range of accommodation options for every type of traveler. Whether you're looking for a comfortable pilgrim hostel or a more luxurious stay, this city has it all:

- **Gallery Hostel**: This boutique hostel is more than just a place to crash. Located in the artsy district, it blends modern design with comfort. The staff is incredibly welcoming, and the rooms—whether shared or private—are impeccably clean and stylish. It's a great spot for pilgrims looking to rest in style without breaking the bank.

- **Porto A.S. 1829 Hotel:** For a more upscale experience, this charming hotel is situated in a historic building, beautifully restored to retain its old-world elegance. The location is ideal for exploring the city, and the attention to detail makes this a standout option for pilgrims looking to treat themselves.

- **The Passenger Hostel:** Located inside Porto's iconic São Bento train station, this hostel is perfect for those who want to be at the heart of Porto's vibrant energy. The interiors are modern and quirky, with spacious dorms and private rooms.

Restaurant Recommendations in Porto

Porto's food scene is a delight, offering everything from traditional Portuguese fare to more contemporary dining options:

- **Cantina 32**: Located near the Ribeira district, this quirky restaurant is known for its playful take on Portuguese classics. From hearty dishes like francesinha (a loaded sandwich unique to Porto) to seafood fresh from the Atlantic, Cantina 32 offers a memorable dining experience.

- **Café Santiago:** If you're eager to try Porto's famous francesinha, Café Santiago is often hailed as one of the best spots in the city. It's a simple, no-frills place, but the food is absolutely comforting—just what a tired pilgrim needs.

- **Taberna dos Mercadores**: For those seeking traditional, home-cooked Portuguese meals, this small restaurant in the Ribeira is a hidden gem. The seafood dishes, particularly the octopus and cod, are local favorites.

Exploring Porto

Once you've settled in, Porto offers plenty to explore. Whether you decide to stay a day or two, there's no shortage of things to see and experience:

- **Ribeira District:** This UNESCO World Heritage site is full of narrow, winding streets that open up to incredible views of the Douro River. It's a great place to wander and get lost, with a new surprise waiting around every corner—whether it's a street performer or a quiet café.

- **Clérigos Tower:** If your legs still have some energy, climbing to the top of this baroque tower rewards you with panoramic views of Porto. It's a steep climb, but the views are worth the effort.

- **Livraria Lello:** One of the world's most beautiful bookstores, Livraria Lello is a must-visit. Its intricate woodwork and grand staircase make it feel more like a movie set than a bookstore.

Porto to Vilarinho

After indulging in Porto's energy, the Camino beckons you onward toward Vilarinho. This stage is about 25 km, offering a pleasant escape from city life back into the quieter rhythm of the countryside. The route from Porto begins with suburban areas but soon opens up to more pastoral landscapes, as the Camino weaves through small villages and rural pathways.

The Path to Vilarinho

Leaving Porto, you'll gradually find yourself back in the peaceful ambiance of the Camino, with green fields and vineyards flanking the route. The journey feels more meditative here, and after the sensory overload of Porto, this return to nature offers a perfect balance. The quiet roads are interrupted only by the occasional sound of birds and distant tractors working the fields.

While the route is not overly challenging, it does require some stamina, especially if you've been on the road for days. Remember to hydrate and take breaks when needed.

Hotel Recommendations in Vilarinho

While Vilarinho is a small village, it offers a few welcoming accommodations for weary pilgrims:

- **Albergue de Peregrinos de Vilarinho:** This simple but cozy albergue is specifically designed with pilgrims in mind. The facilities are basic, but the atmosphere is warm, and the communal dining space encourages conversation and camaraderie among walkers.

- **Casa de Vilarinho de S. Romão**: If you're looking for something a little more comfortable, this rural guesthouse offers a tranquil escape. With beautiful gardens and a traditional stone building, it provides a peaceful spot to relax before continuing your journey.

Restaurant Recommendations in Vilarinho

Dining options in Vilarinho are more limited compared to Porto, but what the village lacks in quantity, it makes up for in quality:

- **Adega Regional de Vilarinho:** This traditional Portuguese restaurant offers hearty, homemade meals at reasonable prices.

Expect dishes like grilled meats, stews, and the ever-present bacalhau (cod), along with a selection of local wines.

- **Café Central**: A simple spot in the heart of the village where you can enjoy a light meal or snack. It's a great place to grab a coffee and a pastry while soaking in the village atmosphere.

These two stages offer contrasting experiences—the industrial outskirts and bustling streets of Porto followed by the quietude of Vilarinho's countryside. This shift is a beautiful reminder of the Camino's dual nature, balancing human history with the simplicity of nature. As you walk through this blend of urban and rural, you'll likely feel a deeper connection to the route, appreciating both the busy energy of the city and the meditative silence of the country roads.

Porto is a place to recharge, enjoy some of the best food and sights Portugal has to offer, and reflect on the journey so far. As you leave it behind and head toward Vilarinho, you step back into the rhythm of the Camino, moving ever closer to Santiago de Compostela.

Chapter 6

Stage 18 - Stage 25

Vilarinho to Barcelos

This stretch of the Camino Portugués, from Vilarinho to Barcelos, unfolds gently as you move through picturesque rural landscapes. The journey is rich in natural beauty, offering pilgrims quiet roads, fields, and occasional villages that break up the solitude. As you approach Barcelos, the scenery intensifies, leading you to one of the most culturally vibrant towns on the Camino.

The distance from Vilarinho to Barcelos is approximately 19 km, a more moderate section of the Camino that allows you to relax while still covering solid ground. The terrain is a mixture of dirt paths, countryside roads, and a few paved sections as you get closer to Barcelos. The combination of nature and small villages makes for a serene experience, but the occasional uphill sections might demand some energy.

Arriving in Barcelos

As you enter Barcelos, you'll find yourself in a town known for its vibrant history, crafts, and, of course, the famous Rooster of Barcelos, a national symbol of Portugal. Barcelos is a lively town, offering a range of shops, restaurants, and attractions that make it an excellent stop for pilgrims seeking a little more than just rest.

Hotel Recommendations

- **Hotel Bagoeira:** Centrally located and offering comfortable rooms at reasonable prices, Hotel Bagoeira is a popular choice for pilgrims. With its traditional Portuguese style and excellent service, it provides everything you need for a restful night.

- **Art'Otel Barcelos**: For something a bit more modern, Art'Otel Barcelos offers stylish rooms with contemporary amenities. Located near the main square, it's ideal for those looking to explore the town easily.

- **Alojamento Local Arantes**: A simpler but clean and cozy option, this guesthouse is perfect for pilgrims seeking affordable accommodation with a welcoming atmosphere. The owner's warm hospitality makes this spot especially memorable.

Restaurant Recommendations

- **Restaurante Turismo:** This restaurant is known for its hearty Portuguese dishes, including the famed Bacalhau à Brás (salted cod with eggs and potatoes) and various grilled meats.

It's an ideal stop for pilgrims looking for filling, authentic meals.

- **Taberna do Armando:** For a more casual meal, this tavern offers local dishes and a great selection of wines. The laid-back atmosphere makes it a perfect place to relax after a day's walk.

- **Café Barcelos**: If you're in need of a lighter meal or just want a coffee and pastry, Café Barcelos is a great option. Located near the town center, it's a bustling spot where locals and pilgrims mingle.

Barcelos to Ponte de Lima

The stretch from Barcelos to Ponte de Lima brings you deeper into the scenic landscapes of northern Portugal, with a beautiful mix of rural paths, rivers, and vineyards. It's one of the most breathtaking sections of the Camino, leading to the historic town of Ponte de Lima, known for its medieval architecture and charming riverfront.

The distance from Barcelos to Ponte de Lima is about 34 km. This is a longer day, but the beauty of the route helps to keep you motivated. The terrain alternates between open fields, forest paths, and country roads. There are some challenging uphill stretches, especially as you approach Ponte de Lima, but the views along the way more than make up for the effort.

Arriving in Ponte de Lima

Arriving in Ponte de Lima feels like walking into a storybook. The town is set on the banks of the Lima River, with its iconic medieval bridge connecting both sides of the town. It's a town rich in history, known for its annual festivals, stunning architecture, and the perfect place for pilgrims to relax after a long day's walk.

Hotel Recommendations

- **Mercearia da Vila:** This boutique hotel is located in the heart of Ponte de Lima, offering stylish rooms that combine modern comfort with traditional charm. It's perfect for pilgrims seeking a bit of luxury after a long day on the road.

- **Hotel Império do Norte:** A comfortable, mid-range option, this hotel provides all the necessary amenities, with the bonus of being right by the river. The view from your room adds an extra layer of tranquility to your stay.

- **Casa das Andorinhas:** For a more intimate, guesthouse-style stay, Casa das Andorinhas offers cozy rooms and personal attention from the hosts. It's a homey spot where you'll feel like more than just another traveler.

Restaurant Recommendations

- **Taberna Cadeia Velha:** This historic tavern offers a fantastic selection of traditional Portuguese dishes, including local specialties like arroz de sarrabulho (a rich rice dish) and lampreia (lamprey eel). Its charming setting in the old town makes it a must-visit.

- **Restaurante Encanada**: Located near the river, this restaurant is known for its relaxed vibe and delicious seafood. From fresh fish to octopus, it's a perfect spot to unwind with a meal that celebrates local flavors.

- **Cantinho da Ramboia:** For a more informal dining experience, this café-restaurant is great for grabbing a light meal or a sandwich. It's popular among pilgrims for its welcoming staff and affordable prices.

What to Do in Ponte de Lima

Once you've arrived in Ponte de Lima, you'll find yourself surrounded by history and natural beauty. After a day of walking, the town invites you to slow down and enjoy its quiet charm:

- **Medieval Bridge**: Ponte de Lima's most iconic feature, the medieval bridge, is a must-see. Take a stroll across the bridge and enjoy views of the Lima River and the surrounding landscape.

- **Jardins do Paço do Marques:** These formal gardens are a peaceful oasis in the town. Perfect for a relaxed afternoon walk, the gardens are filled with beautiful flowers, fountains, and statues.

- **Museu dos Terceiros**: For those interested in history and art, this museum offers a glimpse into the religious and cultural heritage of the region. It's housed in a former convent and is a quiet, reflective space.

These stages of the Camino Portugués are all about contrasts—between the open rural landscapes and the rich history of the towns you pass through. Walking from Vilarinho to Barcelos brings a sense of tranquility, while the journey from Barcelos to Ponte de Lima offers some of the most beautiful scenery you'll encounter on the entire route.

From the crafts and history of Barcelos to the medieval charm of Ponte de Lima, these sections allow pilgrims to experience both the natural and cultural richness of northern Portugal. It's a journey that will challenge you physically but reward you with experiences that linger long after you've left the Camino behind.

Ponte de Lima to Rubiães

The journey from Ponte de Lima to Tui is one of the most beautiful yet challenging sections of the Camino Portugués. With lush landscapes, historical villages, and the crossing into Spain, these stages offer a unique mix of natural beauty and a sense of accomplishment as you move closer to Santiago de Compostela. However, these stages also demand mental and physical strength, as you encounter steeper terrain and longer stretches of solitude. This is a turning point on your Camino—where the experience becomes as much about the journey inward as it is about the path beneath your feet.

Leaving the charming town of Ponte de Lima, you'll be struck by the stunning medieval architecture and the famous Roman Bridge that spans the Lima River. The peaceful scenery offers a gentle start to what will soon be one of the toughest days of your journey. The climb to the Alto da Portela Grande is notoriously steep and rocky, often referred to as the hardest ascent on the Portuguese Camino. But don't let that discourage you—though difficult, it's also breathtaking, with sweeping views of the surrounding valleys and mountains.

The stage is a relatively short one, but the challenge lies in the terrain, not the distance. The steep climbs, particularly after Labruja, can be demanding. Take it slow, rest often, and remember to stay hydrated. The landscape is varied, offering dense forests, ancient stone paths, and moments of serene solitude as you walk through the countryside.

Hotel Recommendations in Rubiães

- **Albergue Constantino AL:** A great choice for pilgrims looking for a simple, comfortable place to stay. This family-run albergue offers clean beds, warm hospitality, and hearty meals. The atmosphere is relaxed and welcoming, perfect for resting after a tough day of walking.

- **Casa das Olas:** For those looking to treat themselves after the demanding climb, Casa das Olas offers a more upscale experience. Set in a beautifully restored historic building, this guesthouse offers cozy rooms and lovely views of the surrounding countryside. The attention to detail and personal touch make it a memorable stop.

Restaurant Recommendations in Rubiães

- **Restaurante O Constantino**: Located near the albergue of the same name, this restaurant offers traditional Portuguese food in generous portions. After a long day on the Camino, their homemade dishes—think bacalhau (codfish) and hearty soups—will replenish your energy for the next stage.

Rubiães to Tui

The walk from Rubiães to Tui is a rewarding one, as it takes you through small villages, quiet countryside, and ultimately across the border into Spain. The stage is relatively easy compared to the previous day's ascent, with gentler hills and more opportunities to relax along the way.

About 7 km into the day's walk, you'll reach Valença, the last town before crossing into Spain. Valença is famous for its imposing fortress, which overlooks the Minho River and offers panoramic views of the surrounding area. It's a lovely place to stop, take a breath, and explore a bit before moving forward.

The crossing into Spain feels significant—not just because you're crossing into another country, but because it marks a major milestone on your Camino. The walk across the International Bridge spanning the Minho River takes you from Valença to Tui, where you'll immediately notice a change in architecture and atmosphere. Tui, with its medieval charm and towering cathedral, is a fitting place to celebrate this important step on your journey.

Hotel Recommendations in Tui

- **Albergue de Peregrinos de Tui:** A popular choice among pilgrims, this albergue is simple but welcoming, providing everything you need for a restful night. The central location makes it easy to explore Tui's old town, and the communal atmosphere offers a chance to connect with fellow pilgrims.

- **Parador de Tui:** For a bit more luxury, the Parador de Tui is a historic hotel set within a stunning medieval building. The rooms are comfortable and spacious, and the ambiance is steeped in history, giving you a taste of traditional Spanish hospitality. After days of albergues, this might feel like an indulgence, but it's well worth it for a special night on the Camino.

Restaurant Recommendations in Tui

- **Tapería O Albergue:** A popular spot with locals and pilgrims alike, this restaurant offers a range of delicious tapas and traditional Spanish dishes. From Galician-style octopus to hearty stews, the food is full of flavor and provides a true taste of the region.

- **O Vello Cabalo Furado:** Located in the heart of Tui, this restaurant serves a mix of traditional and modern Spanish cuisine. The menu highlights fresh, local ingredients, including seafood and meats, and the atmosphere is cozy yet lively—a perfect spot to celebrate your crossing into Spain.

What to Do in Tui

Once you've rested and eaten, take some time to explore Tui. This ancient city is rich with history, and there's no shortage of things to see and do before you head out on the next stage of your journey.

- **Tui Cathedral:** Dating back to the 12th century, Tui's cathedral is a stunning example of Romanesque and Gothic architecture. Climb to the top for impressive views of the town and the surrounding countryside.

- **Fortaleza de Valença:** If you didn't stop to explore Valença's fortress earlier in the day, it's worth doubling back across the bridge to visit. The well-preserved walls and ramparts are not only historically significant but also offer great views of the Minho River.

- **Walk Along the Minho River:** For something a bit more peaceful, take a stroll along the riverbanks. The scenery is beautiful, and the path is less taxing on tired legs, offering a nice way to unwind.

This section of the Camino Português, from Ponte de Lima to Tui, represents a pivotal point in your pilgrimage. The physical challenge of the climb to Rubiães followed by the symbolic crossing into Spain creates a sense of forward momentum—each step bringing you closer to Santiago. The lush landscapes, historical landmarks, and peaceful villages remind you that the Camino is not just a journey of kilometers, but of discovery and transformation.

Whether you're reflecting on your physical progress or contemplating the deeper meaning of the pilgrimage, this stage offers both challenges and rewards in equal measure. By the time you reach Tui, you'll have a renewed sense of purpose and accomplishment, ready to take on the final stages of your Camino with a full heart and lightened spirit.

Tui to O Porriño

Leaving Tui, you cross from Portugal into Spain, marking an exciting milestone on the Camino. This 18-kilometer stretch to O Porriño offers a pleasant, varied walk through small villages, forests, and some industrial areas. Although not the most scenic stage of the Camino, the journey is enriched by the feeling of entering the final country on your pilgrimage.

From Tui to O Porriño, the terrain is generally flat, making it a relatively easy walk compared to some earlier stages. The initial part of the route meanders through forests and farmlands, offering a peaceful atmosphere. However, the last few kilometers lead through the industrial outskirts of O Porriño, which can feel a bit monotonous but is part of the experience.

Highlights Along the Way

- **Tui Cathedral**: Before you leave Tui, take time to visit the impressive Tui Cathedral. This Gothic structure, with its fortified towers, offers a panoramic view of both Spain and Portugal from the rooftop. It's a reminder of the history and spirituality that surround the Camino.

- **San Telmo Chapel:** Another highlight in Tui is the Chapel of San Telmo, dedicated to the patron saint of the town. It's a charming spot to pause and reflect before continuing your walk.

- **Natural Paths:** For much of the journey, you'll find yourself walking along natural pathways flanked by eucalyptus trees and lush greenery. These shaded stretches are especially welcome during warmer days.

Arriving in O Porriño

O Porriño is a small industrial town, and while it doesn't have the historical charm of some other Camino stops, it's a practical place to rest and refresh. Despite its industrial backdrop, O Porriño is welcoming, offering plenty of services for pilgrims, from comfortable accommodations to eateries.

Hotel Recommendations in O Porriño

- **Albergue O Porriño**: This municipal albergue offers basic but clean facilities, ideal for pilgrims looking for an affordable place to stay. It's centrally located, making it easy to access restaurants and shops.

- **Hotel Parque Porriño**: If you're seeking more comfort, this hotel provides cozy rooms and a peaceful setting, just outside the town center. The staff is friendly and often caters to pilgrims.

- **Alojamiento Camino Portugués:** A modern option, this guesthouse offers private rooms with a touch of elegance. It's perfect if you're looking for a restful night in a quieter atmosphere.

Restaurant Recommendations in O Porriño

- **La Cueva:** This small, family-run restaurant offers traditional Galician dishes. The octopus (pulpo) is highly recommended, as is their local seafood. It's a cozy place to enjoy a hearty meal after a long day's walk.

- **Bar Galego**: A casual spot for tapas and drinks, Bar Galego is perfect for a relaxed evening. The prices are reasonable, and it's popular with both locals and pilgrims, giving it a lively atmosphere.

- **Cervecería O Porriño:** If you're in the mood for a lighter meal or a cold drink, this local tavern offers a great selection of snacks, beers, and wines. It's a good place to sit back and unwind with fellow pilgrims.

O Porriño to Redondela

The walk from O Porriño to Redondela, about 15 kilometers, is often seen as a short but varied stage. It takes you from the industrial outskirts of O Porriño back into nature, passing through small rural areas and scenic hilltops. Though the distance isn't far, the landscape adds a sense of adventure and tranquility, and the approach to Redondela is especially scenic.

After leaving the industrial parts of O Porriño, the route gradually ascends, offering beautiful views over the Galician countryside. You'll pass through shaded forest trails and cross the Louro River before a small climb to the Alto de Inxertado, the highest point on this stage. The descent into Redondela offers stunning views of the Ría de Vigo, a picturesque coastal inlet that adds to the charm of this stage.

Highlights Along the Way

- **Alto de Inxertado**: This hill offers some of the most rewarding views of the Galician landscape. The climb isn't too strenuous, but the panorama makes it feel like a high point on the journey.

- **Countryside and Villages:** As you walk, you'll pass small hamlets and agricultural fields, offering a glimpse of rural life in this part of Spain. It's a peaceful walk, and the natural beauty is refreshing after the more urban sections of the Camino.

Arriving in Redondela

Redondela, known as the "town of viaducts," is where the coastal and central routes of the Camino Portugués converge. It's a lively town with plenty of bars, restaurants, and accommodations, making it a popular stop for pilgrims. The town itself is small, but it has a welcoming energy, and the convergence of two Camino routes brings a mix of people and cultures.

Hotel Recommendations in Redondela

- **Albergue Casa da Herba:** Located in the heart of Redondela, this albergue is cozy and well-maintained. It's a favorite among pilgrims due to its central location and friendly staff. The common areas are ideal for sharing stories with fellow walkers.

- **Hotel Antolín**: If you're looking for something a bit more upscale, Hotel Antolín offers rooms with views of the Ría de Vigo. The hotel is a short walk from the center of Redondela, providing a peaceful retreat with a touch of luxury.

- **Albergue A Conserveira**: This modern and colorful albergue is designed with pilgrims in mind. It offers private rooms as well as dormitories, and the outdoor terrace is perfect for relaxing after a day of walking.

Restaurant Recommendations in Redondela

- **Casa Mucha:** This local gem serves traditional Galician dishes with a focus on fresh seafood. Their octopus and grilled fish are highly recommended. The atmosphere is warm, and the service is attentive.

- **O Lar do Mochiño:** For a more contemporary twist on Galician cuisine, O Lar do Mochiño offers a creative menu using local ingredients. Their tapas are particularly good, and it's a great place to enjoy a casual meal with fellow pilgrims.

- **La Barraca:** If you're craving a more relaxed dining experience, La Barraca offers simple but delicious meals in a laid-back environment. It's a great spot for a quick bite or a glass of wine to unwind.

The journey from Tui to Redondela is more than just walking—it's a transformative experience as you move deeper into Spain. Each step brings you closer to Santiago, and while the landscape shifts from industrial outskirts to scenic countryside, the feeling of progress and purpose grows stronger.

This part of the Camino is also filled with small joys, whether it's the quiet moments under the shade of eucalyptus trees, the views over Galician hills, or the first sight of the Ría de Vigo. You'll meet fellow pilgrims who have come from different starting points, and the shared experience of walking towards Santiago creates a special bond.

Redondela to Pontevedra

Leaving Redondela, you embark on a scenic walk that meanders through lush forests and picturesque villages. The path is often shaded by trees, providing a comfortable refuge from the sun as you make your way toward Pontevedra. This stretch of the Camino is not only a feast for the eyes but also a journey filled with the sounds of nature and the occasional laughter of fellow pilgrims.

Highlights Along the Way

- **The Beautiful Ría de Vigo**: As you leave Redondela, you may catch glimpses of the stunning Ría de Vigo, with its sparkling waters and surrounding hills. The sight of boats gently bobbing in the harbor is a calming start to your day.

- **Sampaio**: Just a short distance from Redondela, this charming village invites you to pause. The local church, Igrexa de San Juan, is a quaint spot that's perfect for a quick photo op or a moment of reflection.

- **Nature Trails:** This part of the Camino is rich in natural beauty, featuring lush greenery and tranquil paths. Take a moment to listen to the sounds of birds and rustling leaves as you walk.

Arriving in Pontevedra

When you finally reach Pontevedra, you'll be greeted by a vibrant, pedestrian-friendly city. The town's historic center is a maze of narrow streets lined with charming shops and cozy cafes, making it a delightful place to unwind after your walk.

Hotel Recommendations

- **Hotel Avenida**: Conveniently located near the city center, this comfortable hotel offers modern amenities at reasonable prices. It's a great base for exploring Pontevedra, with friendly staff ready to help you.

- **Hotel Rias Bajas:** Just a short walk from the main square, this hotel features cozy rooms and a lovely terrace. The warm atmosphere makes it a popular choice among pilgrims.

- **Albergue La Peregrina**: If you're looking for a budget-friendly option, this albergue caters specifically to pilgrims. It provides a simple yet welcoming environment and has a communal kitchen for preparing your meals.

Restaurant Recommendations

After a day of walking, indulging in local cuisine is a must:

- **Casa Nené:** A favorite among locals and pilgrims alike, this restaurant offers a fantastic selection of traditional Galician dishes. Try their octopus (pulpo) or the local empanada for an authentic taste of the region.

- **O Portón**: Known for its warm atmosphere and friendly service, this restaurant features a diverse menu with both vegetarian and meat options. Their grilled fish and homemade desserts are particularly popular.

- **Taberna O Rincón:** Located near the main square, this cozy tavern serves delicious tapas and local wines. It's a great spot to relax with fellow travelers and share stories over a meal.

Pontevedra to Caldas de Reis

After a restful night in Pontevedra, it's time to continue your journey toward Caldas de Reis. This leg of the Camino is characterized by a mix of urban landscapes and serene countryside, providing a nice balance that keeps your walk interesting.

Highlights Along the Way

- **A Ponte do Burgo:** Just after leaving Pontevedra, you'll cross this ancient bridge, which offers lovely views of the river and surrounding area. It's a perfect spot to take a moment and soak in the scenery.

- **Vila de Caldas**: As you approach Caldas de Reis, you'll pass through charming hamlets that showcase the traditional architecture of the region. Each small village has its unique character, making the walk feel like a journey through time.

- **Hot Springs:** Caldas de Reis is famous for its thermal baths. As you arrive, you might consider taking a dip in one of the local thermal pools. The soothing waters are a perfect way to relax your tired muscles after a long day of walking.

Arriving in Caldas de Reis

Upon reaching Caldas de Reis, you'll find a town steeped in history, famous for its hot springs and beautiful rivers. The town center is compact, making it easy to explore on foot.

Hotel Recommendations

- **Hotel A Calle:** Located in the heart of Caldas de Reis, this hotel offers comfortable accommodations with friendly service. It's a great choice for those looking for convenience and comfort after a long day of walking.

- **Albergue de Caldas de Reis:** For pilgrims on a budget, this albergue provides a welcoming environment. With shared facilities and a communal kitchen, it's a great place to meet fellow travelers.

Restaurant Recommendations

After you've settled in, treat yourself to a delicious meal:

- **Restaurante O Faiado:** Known for its cozy atmosphere and generous portions, this restaurant serves a range of traditional dishes. Don't miss their local seafood and seasonal vegetables, all prepared with a touch of Galician flair.

- **Pazo de Caldas**: Situated near the thermal baths, this charming eatery specializes in local wines and tapas. The relaxed vibe makes it a great place to unwind and enjoy the local cuisine.

- **Casa de Caldas**: This family-run restaurant offers a selection of homemade dishes using fresh, local ingredients. Their daily specials are a great way to experience the flavors of the region.

Walking from Redondela to Caldas de Reis is a delightful experience that captures the essence of the Camino Portugués. With beautiful landscapes, rich history, and warm hospitality, each step on this stretch allows you to connect with the natural beauty of Galicia and the heartwarming spirit of fellow pilgrims. Whether you're savoring local dishes, soaking in the thermal waters, or simply enjoying the moment, this part of your journey is sure to leave a lasting impression.

Caldas de Reis to Padrón

This segment of the Camino Portugués offers a remarkable blend of natural beauty, rich history, and a sense of culmination as you approach the sacred city of Santiago de Compostela. The route from Caldas de Reis to Padrón and then on to Santiago is filled with charm, picturesque landscapes, and the promise of reaching your destination.

The distance from Caldas de Reis to Padrón is about 19 km. The path winds through lush greenery and gentle hills, providing a refreshing walk that's manageable for most pilgrims. As you make your way along, you'll encounter tranquil streams and vibrant forests, making this stretch feel like a peaceful retreat.

Highlights Along the Way

- **Caldas de Reis**: This small town is famous for its thermal springs. If you have the time, consider taking a relaxing soak in one of the local spas before you head out. The warm waters are a wonderful way to soothe tired muscles after days of walking.

- **The River Ulla**: As you approach Padrón, you'll walk alongside the serene River Ulla, which adds to the tranquil atmosphere of this section. The sound of flowing water and the sights of the surrounding nature create a soothing backdrop for reflection.

Hotel Recommendations in Padrón

Upon reaching Padrón, you'll find a charming town rich in history and culinary delights. Here are a couple of great places to stay:

- **Hotel Pazo de Lestrove**: This beautiful hotel is located in a restored manor house just outside Padrón. Surrounded by gardens, it offers a peaceful retreat with comfortable rooms and a touch of elegance. The warm hospitality and serene atmosphere make it a perfect stop for weary pilgrims.

- **Casa de la Abuela**: A cozy guesthouse right in the heart of Padrón, this charming place provides a homey feel with clean and comfortable rooms. The owners are friendly and often share local tips and recommendations.

Restaurant Recommendations in Padrón

Padrón is known for its delicious cuisine, especially its peppers, which are celebrated throughout Spain. Here are some delightful dining options:

- **Restaurante O Camiño**: A local favorite, this restaurant offers a variety of traditional Galician dishes. Their seafood is particularly noteworthy, and you can't miss trying the pimientos de Padrón—small green peppers that are typically fried and sprinkled with sea salt.

- **Mesón do Bento:** This cozy mesón serves hearty local fare. It's a great spot to refuel after your walk, offering a selection of tapas and filling main courses, including local meats and fresh fish. The atmosphere is warm and welcoming, perfect for pilgrims.

Padrón to Santiago de Compostela

The final leg from Padrón to Santiago is approximately 25 km. This stretch is generally flat, making it a straightforward walk, but with the excitement of nearing your destination, you'll likely feel the energy and anticipation in the air.

Highlights Along the Way

- **The Historic Center of Padrón:** Before leaving, take a moment to explore Padrón's charming streets. The Church of Santiago is worth a visit, famous for its connection to the pilgrimage. Legend has it that the remains of St. James were brought here by boat.

- **The Last Few Kilometers:** As you approach Santiago, the path becomes busier with fellow pilgrims, and the excitement builds. The anticipation of seeing the cathedral draws people together, and the shared experience can be incredibly moving.

Arriving in Santiago de Compostela

As you walk through the streets of Santiago, you'll likely feel a rush of emotions—joy, relief, and perhaps a hint of disbelief that you've completed your journey. The iconic silhouette of the Cathedral of Santiago rises in the distance, a sight that fills the heart with awe.

Hotel Recommendations in Santiago de Compostela

After the long journey, finding a comfortable place to rest is essential. Here are a few options that cater to pilgrims:

- **Hotel Palacio del Carmen:** Set in a converted convent, this hotel exudes history and charm. Located just a short walk from the cathedral, it offers elegant rooms, a beautiful garden, and excellent amenities to ensure a restful stay.

- **Albergue O Camiño:** A popular choice for pilgrims, this albergue offers simple accommodations at budget-friendly prices. The communal atmosphere fosters camaraderie among fellow travelers, and it's a great place to share stories of your journey.

Restaurant Recommendations in Santiago de Compostela

Santiago is renowned for its culinary scene, so take the time to indulge in some local dishes:

- **Casa de Xantar:** This rustic restaurant offers traditional Galician cuisine in a warm and welcoming environment. Don't miss the octopus a la gallega—a must-try dish that captures the essence of the region.

- **Restaurante O Curro da Parra:** For a more upscale dining experience, this restaurant features modern interpretations of classic dishes. The ambiance is sophisticated yet relaxed, perfect for celebrating your journey with a memorable meal.

Walking from Caldas de Reis to Santiago de Compostela is not just about reaching the end; it's a culmination of experiences, friendships, and personal growth. Each step brings you closer not only to the physical destination but also to a deeper understanding of yourself and your journey. The landscapes, the towns, and the people you encounter all contribute to this rich tapestry of experience that stays with you long after you've left the Camino behind.

As you stand before the magnificent Cathedral of Santiago, take a moment to reflect on everything you've accomplished. Embrace the joy, the struggle, and the profound sense of connection that this journey has brought into your life. This final stretch is a celebration of all that has come before, and the memories you've created will be cherished forever.

Chapter 7

The Coastal Route (Porto to Santiago)

Porto to Matosinhos

The Coastal Route of the Camino Portugués is an absolute delight for pilgrims who love the sea. Starting in Porto, you'll feel the vibrant energy of this city before heading north, where the scent of the ocean and the sound of crashing waves guide your steps. The journey from Porto to Matosinhos is a gentle introduction to this scenic route, offering a mix of city charm and coastal beauty.

The distance between Porto and Matosinhos is around 10-12 km, depending on where you start. The walk is relatively easy, following paved roads and pedestrian paths along the coast. It's a perfect first day for those who want to ease into the Camino without rushing.

Highlights Along the Way
- **Ribeira District (Porto):** Before leaving Porto, take a moment to stroll through the Ribeira district. The colorful buildings lining the Douro River, the sound of Fado music drifting from cafes, and the stunning views of the Dom Luís I Bridge make this a perfect spot to pause before beginning your walk.

- **Foz do Douro:** As you leave the heart of Porto, you'll pass through Foz do Douro, where the Douro River meets the

Atlantic Ocean. This stretch of the route is serene, with a long promenade, views of the open sea, and small beaches perfect for a quick rest.

Hotel Recommendations in Matosinhos

After a pleasant walk along the coast, Matosinhos is a great place to rest and recharge. Known for its beaches and seafood, this town is a lovely first stop on the Coastal Route.

- **Hotel Porto Mar:** This hotel offers modern, comfortable rooms just a short walk from the beach. The location is perfect for pilgrims looking to relax after their walk, and the helpful staff can provide local tips and suggestions.

- **Casa do Godinho:** For a more traditional stay, this guesthouse offers a homey atmosphere and friendly service. The rooms are simple but cozy, and the location in central Matosinhos makes it easy to explore the town or head to the beach.

Restaurant Recommendations in Matosinhos

Matosinhos is famous for its seafood, so be sure to treat yourself to some of the freshest fish and shellfish in Portugal. Here are a couple of standout options:

- **Restaurante Lage do Senhor do Padrão**: A local favorite, this restaurant specializes in grilled fish, with a simple yet delicious menu that lets the flavors of the sea shine through. The laid-back ambiance and outdoor seating make it a perfect spot for a post-walk meal.

- **O Gaveto:** For something a bit more refined, O Gaveto is well-known for its seafood dishes, particularly the arroz de marisco (seafood rice). The service is friendly, and the portions are generous—ideal for hungry pilgrims.

Matosinhos to Vila do Conde

Once you've rested in Matosinhos, the next stage of the journey takes you to Vila do Conde, a charming coastal town. This stretch of the Coastal Route is one of the most scenic, with stunning views of the Atlantic Ocean almost the entire way.

The distance from Matosinhos to Vila do Conde is approximately 22-24 km. The walk is mostly flat and follows boardwalks and coastal paths, making it a comfortable but rewarding day. The combination of sandy beaches, fishing villages, and ocean views creates a truly idyllic walking experience.

Highlights Along the Way

- **Leça da Palmeira:** This beach town just north of Matosinhos offers a lovely boardwalk and some incredible views of the Atlantic. If you feel like a short break, the Piscina das Marés, a stunning tidal swimming pool designed by the renowned architect Álvaro Siza, is a unique spot to stop and dip your feet.

- **Mindelo Beach:** A few kilometers further along, you'll pass Mindelo Beach. The long, sandy shoreline and calm waters make it a peaceful place to take a short rest or simply enjoy the ocean breeze.

- **Historic Vila do Conde:** As you approach Vila do Conde, you'll notice the town's historic landmarks, including the Monastery of Santa Clara and the Aqueduct of Vila do Conde, which stretches impressively across the town's landscape. The town itself is a beautiful mix of old-world charm and modern coastal life.

Hotel Recommendations in Vila do Conde

Vila do Conde offers a wide range of accommodations, from budget-friendly pilgrim hostels to more luxurious stays. Here are a couple of good choices for pilgrims:

- **Santana Hotel & Spa:** Located near the river and offering fantastic views of the aqueduct, this hotel provides modern amenities and a relaxing spa—perfect for soothing your muscles after a day of walking.

- **Casa Mindela Farmhouse:** If you're looking for something more unique, this farmhouse is a wonderful choice. It's located just outside of Vila do Conde and offers a quiet, rustic atmosphere with charming rooms and a delicious breakfast.

Restaurant Recommendations in Vila do Conde

Vila do Conde is a foodie's dream, with plenty of fresh seafood and traditional Portuguese dishes to sample. Here are two top picks:

- **Restaurante Caximar:** With its prime location by the sea, Caximar offers a wide variety of seafood dishes. Their caldeirada de peixe (fish stew) is a must-try, and the friendly service adds to the overall experience.

- **Solar do Arco:** For a more traditional Portuguese meal, Solar do Arco offers a welcoming atmosphere and excellent food. Their specialty is grilled meats and seafood, and the cozy interior makes it a perfect place to relax after a long walk.

Walking the Coastal Route from Porto to Matosinhos and then on to Vila do Conde is a deeply rewarding experience, filled with the sounds of the ocean, the warmth of the sun, and the charm of Portugal's coastal towns. Each step brings a unique blend of serenity and excitement as you immerse yourself in both natural beauty and cultural richness.

The journey offers plenty of opportunities to rest, reflect, and enjoy the simple pleasures of life—whether it's a peaceful moment by the sea, a hearty seafood meal, or the friendly conversations with fellow pilgrims and locals alike. These first few days set the tone for the Camino, helping you to unwind and open yourself to the path ahead.

Vila do Conde to Esposende

The distance from Vila do Conde to Esposende is about 23 km. The route is relatively flat and easy to navigate, making it suitable for pilgrims of all levels. You'll follow a mixture of boardwalks, coastal paths, and minor roads as you pass through small seaside villages and natural landscapes.

Highlights Along the Way

- **Vila do Conde:** Before leaving this charming coastal town, take some time to visit the Monastery of Santa Clara and the famous Aqueduct of Vila do Conde. The town is known for its history of shipbuilding, and the waterfront is lined with traditional fishing boats.

- **Beaches and Coastal Views**: The path offers spectacular ocean views, especially in the early morning light. You'll pass by golden sand beaches like Praia de Árvore and Praia da Póvoa de Varzim, perfect spots for a short rest and to take in the sea air.

Hotel Recommendations in Esposende

Esposende, a small coastal town, is an ideal place to rest after a day of walking. Here are a couple of recommended places to stay:

- **Hotel Suave Mar:** Overlooking the ocean, this comfortable hotel provides spacious rooms, a swimming pool, and an excellent on-site restaurant. Its proximity to the beach makes it a peaceful retreat for pilgrims looking to relax after a day on the Camino.

- **Hostel Eleven:** For a more budget-friendly option, Hostel Eleven offers clean, modern accommodations right in the heart of Esposende. The rooftop terrace provides a wonderful view of the town, and the hostel's friendly atmosphere makes it a popular choice for walkers.

Restaurant Recommendations in Esposende

Esposende is known for its fresh seafood, and you won't be disappointed with the dining options here:

- **Restaurante Água Pé:** A local favorite, this restaurant serves a variety of seafood dishes, including grilled fish and shellfish stew. The friendly service and relaxed atmosphere make it a great spot to unwind.

- **Marbelo:** If you're looking for a more casual meal, Marbelo offers a selection of light bites, sandwiches, and seafood plates. It's located near the beach, so you can enjoy the ocean view while dining.

Esposende to Viana do Castelo

The walk from Esposende to Viana do Castelo is about 24 km, and the route takes you through a mix of coastal paths, forests, and quiet villages. While the terrain is still mostly flat, this section introduces a bit more variety in landscapes, with a few rolling hills and forested areas.

Highlights Along the Way

- **Fão and the Cávado River:** Just outside Esposende, you'll cross the Cávado River in the small village of Fão. This is a scenic spot, with views of the estuary and traditional fishing boats.

- **Beaches of Ofir:** The pristine Praia de Ofir beach stretches along much of this route, and you'll walk parallel to it for a while. Its white sands and dunes are a beautiful sight, and if time permits, it's a great place for a rest.

- **Pine Forests and Rivers:** After the beaches, the trail leads through pine forests and rural roads, providing a peaceful contrast to the coastal scenery.

Arriving in Viana do Castelo

As you approach Viana do Castelo, you'll be greeted by one of the most beautiful cities on the northern Portuguese coast. Known for its rich history and stunning architecture, this city is a gem on the Camino.

Hotel Recommendations in Viana do Castelo

Viana do Castelo has a range of accommodations to suit every pilgrim's needs:

- **Pousada de Viana do Castelo:** For those seeking a more luxurious stay, this beautiful hotel is located on a hill overlooking the city and the ocean. The panoramic views are stunning, and the elegant rooms provide a perfect retreat after your day's walk.

- **Hotel Rali Viana:** A more budget-friendly option, this hotel offers comfortable rooms, a swimming pool, and a central location close to the city's main attractions.

Restaurant Recommendations in Viana do Castelo

The culinary scene in Viana do Castelo is a highlight of this stop, with plenty of traditional Portuguese dishes to try:

- **O Laranjeira:** This charming restaurant is known for its bacalhau (salted cod) dishes, which are a staple of Portuguese cuisine. The cozy interior and friendly staff make it a great place to enjoy a hearty meal after your walk.

- **Tasquinha da Linda:** Located near the riverfront, this family-run restaurant offers fresh seafood and stunning views of the Lima River. Their grilled sardines and octopus rice are particularly popular.

Walking from Vila do Conde to Viana do Castelo along the Coastal Route is a deeply rewarding experience. The rhythm of the ocean, the picturesque villages, and the ever-present sound of the waves create a tranquil atmosphere that allows for reflection and contemplation. Unlike the hustle of inland routes, the Coastal Camino offers a slower, more meditative pace, where nature and the sea become your companions.

As you reach Viana do Castelo, there's a sense of accomplishment but also anticipation for the journey that lies ahead. The Camino is not just about reaching Santiago; it's about the path, the people you meet, and the experiences that unfold with every step.

Viana do Castelo to Caminha

The Coastal Route of the Camino Português is a stunning alternative to the Central Route, offering breathtaking ocean views, cool sea breezes, and a unique coastal culture. The stretch from Viana do Castelo to Caminha and then crossing into Spain from Caminha to A Guarda is a captivating journey, filled with charming seaside towns, dramatic cliffs, and peaceful beaches.

This section covers approximately 28 km, making it a full day of walking. While the terrain is mostly flat, the journey offers a diverse experience, with coastal paths, riverside trails, and small forested areas to keep things interesting.

Highlights Along the Way

- **Viana do Castelo**: Before setting out, take some time to explore Viana do Castelo, one of the most beautiful cities along the coast. Its historic center is full of elegant buildings, including the stunning Basílica de Santa Luzia, which sits atop a hill overlooking the city. The views from the top are nothing short of spectacular and are worth the climb.

- **Praia de Afife:** As you head out of Viana do Castelo, you'll soon pass Afife Beach, one of the most scenic spots along the coast. If you're lucky, you might catch surfers riding the Atlantic waves. The beach itself is a great spot for a rest, with long stretches of sand and the endless horizon of the ocean.

- **Ancient Villages and Churches:** As you continue, the trail meanders through small villages and past charming chapels, such as Igreja de São Pedro de Carreço, each with its own quiet beauty. These peaceful locations invite moments of reflection and offer a slower pace compared to the bustle of city life.

Hotel Recommendations in Caminha

When you reach Caminha, a delightful coastal town with narrow streets and an old-world charm, you'll be ready to relax. Here are a couple of excellent lodging options:

- **Design & Wine Hotel:** This quirky, modern hotel is located near the ferry terminal in Caminha, offering a mix of contemporary design and local tradition. Its comfortable rooms and playful interior design make it a refreshing place to stay, and it offers fantastic views of the Minho River.

- **Hotel Porta do Sol Conference Center & Spa:** Located on the outskirts of Caminha, this hotel provides a more luxurious experience. It features a full-service spa, swimming pools, and spacious rooms with views of the river and the sea—perfect for recharging after a long day of walking.

Restaurant Recommendations in Caminha

Caminha has plenty of excellent dining options, especially if you're looking to indulge in fresh seafood:

- **Restaurante O Muralha:** This local favorite is known for its seafood, offering up dishes like arroz de marisco (seafood rice) and freshly grilled fish. The atmosphere is warm and inviting, and the staff are happy to share their knowledge of the region's specialties.

- **Casa das Velhas:** A cozy spot that specializes in regional dishes, Casa das Velhas is the perfect place to savor traditional Portuguese food, from hearty bacalhau (salted cod) to tender roast lamb. The intimate setting makes for a great way to unwind and enjoy a leisurely meal.

Chapter 8

Stage 6 - Stage 11

Caminha to A Guarda

The journey from Caminha to A Guarda involves crossing into Spain, with a total distance of about 13 km. The standout feature of this leg is the ferry ride across the River Minho, which separates Portugal and Spain. The walk is relatively easy, with coastal trails leading into the Spanish region of Galicia.

Highlights Along the Way

- **The River Minho Crossing**: The ferry from Caminha to A Guarda is a unique part of the Camino experience. As you board the small boat and cross the calm waters of the Minho, you leave Portugal behind and arrive in Galicia. The ride is short but offers beautiful views of the surrounding countryside and the sea.

- **Monte Santa Trega**: As you arrive in A Guarda, don't miss the opportunity to visit Monte Santa Trega, an ancient hilltop settlement with Celtic origins. The site offers panoramic views of the Atlantic Ocean and the river valley, giving you a sense of the long history that predates the Camino itself.

- **A Guarda**: This charming fishing town marks your arrival in Spain. A Guarda is known for its maritime heritage and boasts a relaxed atmosphere, with colorful fishing boats dotting the harbor. The town is perfect for a peaceful stroll, with narrow streets leading to the town's bustling market square.

Hotel Recommendations in A Guarda

Once you reach A Guarda, you'll find several options to rest and recover:

- **Hotel Vila da Guarda:** A comfortable hotel located near the town center, Vila da Guarda offers clean and spacious rooms. It's within walking distance of the port and the town's main attractions, making it a convenient choice for pilgrims.

- **Hotel Convento de San Benito**: This unique hotel is set in a converted convent, offering an atmospheric stay with a mix of history and modern comfort. The cloistered setting is peaceful and serene, ideal for a restful night before continuing your pilgrimage.

Restaurant Recommendations in A Guarda

Seafood lovers will find themselves in heaven in A Guarda, which is famous for its lobster and shellfish:

- **Restaurante Xeito**: This cozy eatery is beloved by locals for its fresh seafood dishes. Try the lobster stew, a specialty of A Guarda, or the pulpo a la gallega—a Galician-style octopus dish that's tender and delicious.

- **Marisquería Bahía**: Situated along the waterfront, this restaurant is perfect for enjoying seafood with a view. Their grilled razor clams and crab dishes are highly recommended, and the outdoor seating lets you soak in the fresh ocean air while dining.

The walk from Viana do Castelo to A Guarda is one that awakens the senses. The salty sea breeze, the sound of waves crashing along the shore, and the ever-changing scenery make this part of the Camino truly unique. The coastal route offers a connection to both nature and history, with every step bringing you closer to Spain and the final destination of Santiago de Compostela.

As you cross the River Minho and leave Portugal behind, you'll feel the excitement of entering a new chapter of your pilgrimage. The transition from the Portuguese to the Spanish landscape is both symbolic and scenic, setting the stage for the final stages of your journey. Whether you choose to rest in Caminha or A Guarda, the warmth of these coastal towns will leave a lasting impression, filling your Camino with memories of sun, sea, and camaraderie.

A Guarda to Baiona

The walk from A Guarda to Baiona covers about 33 km, making it a fairly long but rewarding stretch. The route takes you along coastal paths and boardwalks, with the gentle sound of the waves often accompanying you. The terrain is mostly flat, but be prepared for a few gentle hills as you make your way through coastal forests and seaside towns.

Highlights Along the Way

- **A Guarda:** Before setting off, take some time to visit the Monte Santa Trega. The climb up may be steep, but the panoramic views of the Atlantic Ocean and the mouth of the Miño River are well worth the effort. The hilltop also hosts ancient Celtic ruins, adding a layer of history to your journey.

- **Oia Monastery:** As you continue toward Baiona, you'll come across the ancient Monastery of Oia. Sitting right by the sea, this 12th-century monastery is an iconic sight along the coastal route. Though no longer active, its rugged beauty speaks volumes of its historical significance.

Hotel Recommendations in Baiona

Baiona is a charming coastal town known for its history, medieval architecture, and scenic beauty. After a long walk, here are some great places to rest:

- **Parador de Baiona:** This luxurious hotel, housed in an old fortress, offers stunning views of the Atlantic Ocean. With its thick stone walls, sprawling grounds, and historical ambiance, it feels like a retreat into a different time. The rooms are well-appointed, and the service is excellent—perfect for pilgrims looking for a touch of comfort.

- **Hotel Anunciada:** For a more modest option, Hotel Anunciada is a great choice. It's right in the center of town, close to the harbor, and offers clean, comfortable rooms with warm hospitality. Its central location makes it easy to explore Baiona's attractions on foot.

Restaurant Recommendations in Baiona

Baiona is also known for its wonderful food, especially fresh seafood. Here are some top spots to dine:

- **Restaurante O Burato:** This small, cozy restaurant is a favorite among locals. Their seafood dishes are fantastic, especially the pulpo a la gallega (Galician-style octopus) and the caldeirada (Galician fish stew). The portions are generous, and the flavors are rich.

- **La Boquería de Baiona:** For a more modern dining experience, La Boquería de Baiona offers a range of tapas and seafood with a creative twist. Their seafood platters are beautifully presented and perfect for sharing, while the atmosphere is laid-back but chic.

Baiona to Vigo

The distance from Baiona to Vigo is around 24 km. This section is shorter and continues along the coast, with incredible views of the Cíes Islands in the distance. The path is a mix of paved roads, coastal boardwalks, and sandy trails, all with the sea as your constant companion.

Highlights Along the Way

- Vila Nova de Cerveira: Before you leave Baiona, consider a detour to the town of Vila Nova de Cerveira, a little inland gem known for its medieval castle and vibrant art scene. It adds a cultural flair to your coastal journey.

- Views of the Cíes Islands: As you approach Vigo, the sight of the Cíes Islands comes into view. These islands, part of the Atlantic Islands of Galicia National Park, are a natural paradise and have been dubbed the "Galician Caribbean" for their crystal-clear waters and pristine beaches. Though you won't visit them directly on this route, their beauty from afar adds to the magic of the coastal walk.

Hotel Recommendations in Vigo

Vigo, the largest city in Galicia, is a bustling port town with plenty of accommodations to suit every traveler:

- Gran Hotel Nagari Boutique & Spa: For those seeking some luxury after a long trek, this hotel offers stylish rooms and a rooftop pool with stunning views over the estuary. The spa services here are a perfect way to relax and rejuvenate.

- Hotel Puerta del Sol: A more budget-friendly option, Hotel Puerta del Sol offers comfortable rooms with friendly service.

Located in the heart of Vigo, it's just a short walk to the waterfront, shops, and restaurants.

Restaurant Recommendations in Vigo

Vigo is renowned for its seafood, thanks to its position as one of the most important fishing ports in Europe. Here's where you can savor the best local flavors:

- **O Rei Pescador**: For a classic Galician seafood experience, O Rei Pescador is unbeatable. The fresh catch of the day is presented with simple, traditional preparation, allowing the natural flavors to shine. Their seafood paella is a must-try, rich with the flavors of the sea.

- **Maruja Limón:** For something more contemporary, Maruja Limón is a Michelin-starred restaurant that brings creativity and innovation to Galician cuisine. Each dish is artfully prepared, with local ingredients elevated in unique ways. It's a great spot to celebrate a special milestone in your journey.

Walking the coastal path from A Guarda to Baiona and then on to Vigo brings you closer to the natural beauty of the Galician coastline, while also offering moments of historical intrigue and culinary delight. The gentle rhythm of the ocean, the sweeping views, and the charming towns along the way create an experience that's as serene as it is invigorating.

This section is ideal for pilgrims who appreciate the beauty of nature and the sea, and who want to take their time absorbing the cultural richness of Galicia. Whether you're relaxing in Baiona's medieval fortress or indulging in fresh seafood in Vigo, these days on the coast will leave you with memories that are as vivid as the colors of the Atlantic waters.

Vigo to Redondela

The leg from Vigo to Redondela covers about 16 km. It's a relatively short and gentle stretch, with both urban and rural elements. You'll start in the bustling port city of Vigo and gradually make your way into more peaceful countryside, passing through small villages and shaded paths.

Highlights Along the Way

- **Vigo**: Before leaving Vigo, take some time to explore its lively streets. Vigo is a large, modern city, famous for its seafood and the Ría de Vigo, a stunning estuary. It's well worth enjoying a meal by the waterfront before you set out.

- **O Castro Park:** If you're staying in Vigo the night before, consider hiking up to O Castro for panoramic views of the city and the Atlantic Ocean. The park itself is a peaceful retreat with gardens and ancient ruins.

- **The Walk into Redondela:** As you leave Vigo, the path transitions to more tranquil countryside. The forests along this route provide a pleasant break from the city, and the sight of Redondela's iconic train viaducts will let you know you're nearing your destination.

Hotel Recommendations in Redondela

Once you arrive in Redondela, you'll find several quaint accommodations suited for pilgrims:

- **Albergue Casa da Herba**: A well-maintained and welcoming albergue located in the heart of Redondela. It's popular among pilgrims for its cleanliness and friendly staff, providing a cozy and affordable place to rest after a day of walking.

- **Hotel Antolín:** Located just outside Redondela, right by the estuary, this charming hotel offers stunning water views and a peaceful atmosphere. The rooms are simple but comfortable, and the location gives you a tranquil escape from the town's center.

Restaurant Recommendations in Redondela

Redondela may be a small town, but it's packed with local Galician flavors. Here are a couple of options for a satisfying meal:

- **Casa Mucha:** A local favorite, offering traditional Galician dishes. Try their caldo gallego, a hearty soup that's perfect for replenishing your energy after a long walk. The cozy atmosphere and generous portions make it a great spot to relax.

- **Restaurante O Recanto**: Located near the town center, this restaurant serves a variety of seafood dishes, with the pulpo a la gallega (Galician-style octopus) being a standout. The restaurant's simple decor and homestyle cooking are well-loved by locals and pilgrims alike.

Redondela to Pontevedra

The walk from Redondela to Pontevedra is about 18 km. This stretch takes you deeper into Galicia's lush, rolling hills and picturesque landscapes. The terrain is a mix of paved paths, forested trails, and rural roads, with some gentle hills but nothing too strenuous.

Highlights Along the Way

- **Puente Sampaio**: One of the highlights of this route is crossing the Puente Sampaio, an ancient stone bridge spanning the Verdugo River. This is a peaceful and scenic spot, offering views of the calm waters and surrounding greenery. It's a great place to take a break and enjoy the tranquility of the area.

- **Pontevedra**: As you approach the historic city of Pontevedra, the path takes you through vineyards, farms, and charming hamlets. The old town of Pontevedra is one of the most beautiful and well-preserved in Galicia, known for its pedestrian-friendly streets and vibrant squares.

Hotel Recommendations in Pontevedra

Pontevedra is a larger city with more accommodation options, making it an ideal place to stop for the night. Here are a few recommendations:

- **Parador de Pontevedra:** This luxurious parador is located in a former Renaissance palace in the heart of the city. It offers elegant rooms, a lovely garden, and a touch of history, making it a special place to stay if you're looking to treat yourself after days of walking.

- **Hotel Virgen del Camino**: A more affordable option, this hotel is conveniently located near the old town and offers clean, comfortable rooms. It's a practical and welcoming choice for pilgrims seeking a restful night.

Restaurant Recommendations in Pontevedra

Pontevedra's food scene is a delightful blend of traditional Galician cuisine and more contemporary offerings. Here are a couple of great dining options:

- **Eirado da Leña:** Located in one of Pontevedra's charming squares, this Michelin-starred restaurant offers modern Galician cuisine with an emphasis on fresh, local ingredients.

It's an excellent choice if you're in the mood for something refined and creative, making it a memorable dining experience.

- **Casa Fidel:** For a more laid-back and traditional meal, Casa Fidel serves up classic Galician fare in a relaxed setting. Their empanadas and seafood dishes are particularly popular, and the friendly service will make you feel right at home.

Walking from Vigo to Redondela and Redondela to Pontevedra gives you a taste of the diversity of Galicia, from bustling urban areas to quiet rural landscapes. The changing scenery keeps things interesting, while the shorter distances make these stages feel manageable. The sense of history along the route, especially crossing ancient bridges like the Puente Sampaio, connects you to the countless pilgrims who have walked this way before.

As you explore Pontevedra, the beauty of the old town and the warmth of its people create a sense of arrival and fulfillment. The walk may be physically tiring, but the cultural richness and natural beauty of these stages provide a reward at every turn. The small villages, historic bridges, and the vibrancy of Galician life make this part of the Camino a uniquely enriching experience. Whether you're staying in simple albergues or indulging in the luxury of a parador, each night brings the chance to rest and reflect on the road behind and the journey still ahead.

See The Pontevedra journey of the Central Region
P.150

Chapter 9

Exploring Santiago de Compostela

Arriving in Santiago de Compostela is an emotional moment for pilgrims who have traversed miles of beautiful landscapes, shared countless stories, and forged new friendships along the way. The city, vibrant with life yet rooted in centuries of spiritual history, is not just the end of your journey—it's the beginning of something profound. As you wander through the stone streets, the sound of distant bells and the sight of fellow pilgrims create a deep sense of connection to something greater than yourself.

At the heart of it all stands the Cathedral of Santiago, the crown jewel of the city and the final destination for pilgrims walking the Camino. It is not just a building, but a symbol of hope, faith, and unity for people from all walks of life.

The Cathedral of Santiago

History and Architecture of the Cathedral

The Cathedral of Santiago de Compostela is one of the most important religious landmarks in Europe, attracting millions of pilgrims and visitors every year. Construction of the cathedral began in 1075, and its imposing Romanesque structure has since been influenced by Gothic, Baroque, and Plateresque styles over the centuries. The result is a breathtaking combination of architectural grandeur and historical depth.

The cathedral was built to honor St. James the Greater, one of the twelve apostles of Jesus Christ. Legend has it that his remains were discovered in Galicia, and the cathedral was erected to house his tomb. Over the centuries, the Cathedral has become the symbolic endpoint of the Camino de Santiago, a pilgrimage route that dates back to the Middle Ages.

As you stand in front of the Pórtico da Gloria, the grand western entrance, you'll feel the weight of history around you. The intricate carvings depict scenes from the Bible, welcoming pilgrims with a glimpse of paradise. Once inside, the vastness of the cathedral overwhelms your senses. The soaring columns, arches, and richly adorned chapels offer a space of reflection and awe.

One of the cathedral's most iconic features is the Baroque facade, completed in the 18th century, which faces the Praza do Obradoiro. It's from here that you'll experience that iconic moment—standing in the main square with the cathedral rising before you, knowing you've made it to your destination.

The Botafumeiro: What to Expect at the Pilgrim's Mass

A highlight for many pilgrims visiting the cathedral is the chance to witness the Botafumeiro in action during the Pilgrim's Mass. The Botafumeiro is a massive incense burner, one of the largest in the world, weighing over 80 kilograms and measuring around 1.5 meters in height.

During the Pilgrim's Mass, the Botafumeiro is swung across the transept of the cathedral by a group of eight men known as the tiraboleiros. The sight of this giant censer flying through the air, leaving a trail of incense smoke, is mesmerizing. Originally, the use of the Botafumeiro was practical—it was believed to purify the air in the cathedral after the arrival of hundreds of tired and often unwashed pilgrims. Today, it serves as a powerful symbol of the spiritual journey, a reminder of the collective faith of those who have traveled from all over the world to reach this sacred place.

The Pilgrim's Mass is held daily, typically at 12:00 PM, and welcomes all visitors, whether or not they've walked the Camino. Before the mass begins, you'll hear a roll call of the different nationalities of pilgrims who've completed the journey—a deeply moving moment that makes you feel part of something much larger than yourself.

Though the Botafumeiro is not swung at every mass (it's reserved for special occasions or can be arranged for a fee), witnessing it in motion is an unforgettable experience that adds to the emotional gravity of reaching Santiago.

Visiting the Tomb of St. James

Perhaps the most sacred part of your visit to the cathedral is the opportunity to see the Tomb of St. James, which lies beneath the high altar. Pilgrims come from all corners of the earth to pay their respects at this holy site, believed to house the remains of the apostle James.

To visit the tomb, you'll descend into a crypt, a quiet and reflective space where pilgrims often kneel or offer silent prayers. The silver casket containing the remains is displayed within an ornate chamber. Whether you come here out of faith, curiosity, or a sense of tradition, there's a palpable feeling of reverence in the air.

After visiting the tomb, many pilgrims also participate in the traditional embrace of the Santo dos Croques—a statue of St.

James located behind the high altar. This act, where pilgrims place their hands on the shoulders of the statue, is symbolic of the connection between the apostle and those who have walked in his name.

Exploring Santiago de Compostela, especially the Cathedral of Santiago, is much more than a simple tourist visit. It is a deeply personal and spiritual experience. The history, the architecture, the rituals—everything about the cathedral speaks to centuries of faith, pilgrimage, and the shared human desire for meaning and connection.

As you leave the cathedral, having seen the Botafumeiro swing, visited the tomb, and embraced the statue of St. James, there's a sense of both closure and new beginnings. Whether your Camino was walked for spiritual, physical, or personal reasons, arriving in Santiago offers a profound sense of accomplishment and reflection.

Santiago de Compostela is a place where past and present intertwine, where each pilgrim leaves a trace of their journey in the ancient stones of the cathedral, and where the future feels wide open—filled with hope, gratitude, and the lessons learned on the path.

Receiving the Compostela

The Compostela is a centuries-old tradition, awarded to those who've walked the Camino for spiritual or religious reasons. It's more than just a piece of paper; for many pilgrims, it represents the culmination of not only physical effort but also a deeper inner journey. Whether your motivation was religious, personal reflection, or simply the challenge, holding the Compostela in your hands is a powerful moment of accomplishment.

How to Claim Your Compostela Certificate

Claiming your Compostela is a straightforward process, but there are a few steps and some criteria you'll need to meet:

1. Visit the Pilgrim's Office: The Pilgrim's Office, located at Rúa das Carretas, 33, is where you'll go to receive your certificate. It's usually busy with pilgrims arriving each day, so be prepared for a possible wait, especially during peak season (summer months). The office is well-organized, and you'll often find friendly volunteers and staff ready to help you navigate the process.

2. Present Your Credencial: To claim your Compostela, you'll need to present your Credencial—the pilgrim passport you've been stamping along your journey. Make sure it's stamped at least twice per day during the last 100 kilometers if you're walking, or the last 200 kilometers if you cycled the route. These stamps can be collected at hostels, churches, cafés, or official Camino points.

3. Filling Out a Form: Once you're at the office, you'll be asked to fill out a short form. The staff will check your Credencial to ensure you've met the minimum distance requirements and adhered to the pilgrimage's spirit.

4. Choosing the Language: The Compostela is traditionally written in Latin, so your name will be Latinized, giving it a classical feel. You can request how you'd like it to appear, which adds a special touch to this meaningful certificate.

5. The Compostela Itself: The certificate itself is beautifully crafted, with calligraphy that acknowledges your journey as a pilgrim. It references your completion of the Camino for spiritual reasons, whether religious or based on personal reflection.

Other Pilgrim Certificates Available

In addition to the traditional Compostela, there are other certificates you might be interested in depending on your Camino experience.

- **Certificate of Distance:** For those who want an official record of the total distance walked, the Certificate of Distance provides an additional memento. It's a detailed document that includes the starting point of your Camino and the exact number of kilometers you've covered. This is a great keepsake for those who've walked longer sections or completed more than one route.

- **Compostela for Non-Religious Pilgrims**: If your reasons for walking the Camino were not specifically religious or spiritual but more about personal growth or challenge, you can still receive a non-religious version of the Compostela. This certificate acknowledges your effort and journey without reference to religious motivations.

- **"Finisterra" and "Muxía" Certificates:** For those who continue on the Camino Finisterre or the Camino to Muxía, additional certificates can be earned. These routes take you to the Atlantic coast, where in ancient times, pilgrims believed they'd reached the "end of the world." The journey to these places is a symbolic extension of the Camino and offers an even deeper sense of completion for those who choose to continue beyond Santiago.

Savoring the Moment

Once you've received your Compostela, take a moment to reflect on your journey. You may want to attend the Pilgrim's Mass in the cathedral, where the atmosphere is filled with shared emotions from hundreds of pilgrims like yourself. Whether the Botafumeiro swings or not, being part of the Mass is a moving experience, bringing your Camino full circle.

Walking the Camino isn't just about arriving in Santiago; it's about every step you took to get there. Receiving the Compostela is a way to mark this incredible achievement, but the real reward is often the memories, the personal discoveries, and the fellow pilgrims you met along the way. Santiago offers many moments of reflection, whether it's sitting quietly in the Praza do Obradoiro or wandering through the cobblestone streets of this ancient city. Here, every pilgrim's story intertwines with the legacy of centuries past, creating something timeless and beautiful.

Now, as you hold your Compostela in hand, you can look back at the journey that brought you to this point—each town, each stretch of path, and each challenge along the way is now a part of your personal Camino story.

Chapter 10

Day Trip from Santiago

After taking time to soak in the beauty of Santiago de Compostela, many travelers feel the pull of the rugged Galician coast. Just a short distance from the city, these two day trips—Finisterre and Muxía—offer a chance to continue reflecting, relaxing, and taking in Galicia's wild beauty.

Finisterre

Known as the "**end of the world**", Finisterre (or Fisterra in Galician) was once believed to be the westernmost point of the known world, where the earth stopped and the endless sea began. This windswept cape, just 90 km from Santiago, draws visitors who want to stand at the edge of Europe and gaze into the vast Atlantic Ocean. For many pilgrims, it's a powerful extension of the Camino, a way to symbolically complete the journey by the sea.

The road to Finisterre takes you through breathtaking landscapes of rugged cliffs, rolling hills, and traditional fishing villages. It's a region where the rhythm of life feels slower, and the connection to nature is palpable. The journey ends at the Faro de Finisterre (Finisterre Lighthouse), perched high on rocky cliffs. Here, you can stand and watch the waves crash against the rocks, while the sea stretches endlessly into the horizon. Many pilgrims participate in a time-honored tradition by leaving behind an item of clothing, symbolizing the end of one journey and the start of another.

Before heading back to Santiago, take a moment to stroll through the town of Finisterre itself. It's a small, quiet place, where fishing boats bob in the harbor, and local restaurants serve up some of the freshest seafood you'll ever taste.

- **Restaurant Recommendation**: Tira do Cordel is the place to go for seafood in Finisterre. Their grilled fish, especially the lubina (sea bass), is legendary, and the sea views from the terrace make for a perfect coastal dining experience.

Muxía

Not far from Finisterre lies the coastal town of Muxía, a hidden gem known for its untamed beauty and deep-rooted legends. While not as famous as Finisterre, Muxía has its own powerful allure. Many pilgrims opt to walk here after Santiago or combine it with a trip to Finisterre. The landscape here feels even wilder—dramatic cliffs, crashing waves, and the ever-present roar of the Atlantic.

The town is home to the Santuario da Virxe da Barca, a striking stone church that seems to blend into the rocky coastline. According to local legend, the Virgin Mary appeared here on a stone boat to encourage Saint James as he preached in the area. The stones around the church are said to be part of that boat, and one, the Pedra de Abalar, is believed to have magical properties.

Muxía is a place where the elements take center stage—earth, stone, and sea collide in an awe-inspiring spectacle. The rugged coastline here offers a perfect backdrop for quiet reflection, and the town's slow pace makes it an ideal spot to unwind after the pilgrimage.

- **Restaurant Recommendation**: A de Lolo is a cozy, family-run spot offering traditional Galician dishes with an emphasis on fresh, local seafood. Be sure to try their octopus and razor clams, and enjoy the laid-back atmosphere that Muxía exudes.

Both Finisterre and Muxía are more than just destinations—they're continuations of the Camino experience. Visiting these coastal towns after Santiago offers a chance to reflect on the journey in a different way. While Santiago marks the spiritual completion, standing on the cliffs of Finisterre or walking along the rocky shore of Muxía brings a sense of closure to the physical journey.

These day trips are not just for pilgrims, though. Even if you haven't walked the Camino, the powerful beauty of these locations draws people in. Whether it's the feeling of standing at the edge of the world in Finisterre or witnessing the wildness of the Galician coast in Muxía, these places evoke a sense of awe that lingers long after you've left.

Getting There

Both Finisterre and Muxía are easily accessible from Santiago by bus, car, or as part of a guided tour. Many visitors choose to rent a car for a more flexible day trip, giving them the chance to stop in smaller coastal villages along the way. The journey to

Finisterre typically takes around 1.5 to 2 hours, while Muxía is slightly shorter at around 1.5 hours.

For those wanting a bit more of the Camino experience, there are walking routes that extend from Santiago to both Finisterre and Muxía. This extension adds about 3 to 5 days to the pilgrimage and offers a quieter, more reflective journey along the rugged Galician coast.

In Santiago, you may feel that you've reached the end of your journey, but with these day trips, you'll realize that the journey always continues. Finisterre and Muxía offer a final chance to embrace the freedom and simplicity that the Camino inspires—a place to stand still and look out into the great unknown, and just maybe, feel a deeper sense of what it all means.

Returning Home from Santiago

After days, weeks, or even months of walking, arriving in Santiago de Compostela is an emotional and deeply rewarding experience. The towering spires of the cathedral that have drawn pilgrims for centuries finally come into view, and as you walk into the city, you might feel an overwhelming sense of achievement, relief, or even disbelief that the journey has come to an end. For many, the arrival at the Praza do Obradoiro feels like the culmination of something far greater than just a long walk. But what happens once you've completed your pilgrimage? Returning home after the Camino is a significant part of the experience—one that deserves its own reflection and preparation.

The Mixed Emotions of Finishing

Reaching Santiago is both a momentous occasion and, for some, a bittersweet one. After the constant rhythm of walking day after day, a part of you may feel unsettled by the abrupt end. The camaraderie of fellow pilgrims, the daily simplicity of life on the road, and the physical act of walking have all become part of your routine. Leaving this behind can stir up a mix of emotions—happiness, relief, nostalgia, and even sadness.

Many pilgrims describe the return home as a reverse culture shock. The hustle and bustle of daily life can feel overwhelming after the peaceful rhythm of the Camino. You may find that people back home don't quite understand the significance of your journey or the lessons you've learned along the way. This is normal. It's important to give yourself time to process the experience and adjust to life after the Camino.

Practicalities: Getting Home from Santiago

Once you've spent time celebrating your arrival in Santiago, it's time to think about the practical side of heading home. Santiago de Compostela is well-connected, though you may need to plan your departure carefully, depending on where you are headed next.

- **By Air:** Santiago's Lavacolla Airport is about 20 minutes from the city center and offers direct flights to major cities across Spain and some international destinations. If you're flying further afield, you may need to connect through Madrid or Barcelona. There are shuttle buses from the city to the airport, or you can easily arrange a taxi.

- **By Train:** Spain's railway network, RENFE, offers train services from Santiago to other Spanish cities. If you're traveling within Spain or to a nearby European destination, this can be a comfortable and scenic option. The train station is within walking distance from the city center.

- **By Bus:** Santiago's bus station offers routes to various cities in Spain and Portugal. This can be a more budget-friendly way to travel, though the journey times are longer than by train or plane. Buses are frequent, and tickets can be booked in advance or at the station.

- **Shipping Your Gear Home:** If you've acquired souvenirs or want to lighten your load for the trip home, you might consider shipping some of your belongings back. Many post offices in Santiago offer this service, which can be handy, especially for items like trekking poles that may not fit in carry-on luggage.

The Pilgrim's Certificate: Bringing Home More than Memories

One of the most tangible rewards for completing the Camino is the Compostela, the official certificate of completion, which you can collect from the Pilgrim's Office in Santiago. This beautiful document, written in Latin, is more than just a souvenir—it's a symbol of your achievement and a reminder of the journey you've undertaken.

For many pilgrims, bringing home the Compostela is a cherished part of the experience. You may want to frame it or display it somewhere meaningful as a personal memento of your pilgrimage. Don't forget that you can also receive a certificate of distance if you've walked more than 100 km or cycled more than 200 km, which adds an extra layer of recognition for your efforts.

Post-Camino Reflection and Integration

The Camino doesn't necessarily end when you reach Santiago. For many, the journey continues well after they've returned home. The lessons learned, the people met, and the challenges overcome can leave a lasting impression. The sense of purpose and clarity you may have found on the Camino can shift once you're back in the fast-paced world. But integrating these reflections into your daily life can bring new meaning to your post-Camino journey.

- **Journaling**: If you kept a journal during your walk, revisiting your notes can help you process your experience. Writing down how you felt upon returning home, any struggles you might be facing, or the ways you want to bring the Camino spirit into your everyday life can be a grounding exercise.

- **Staying Connected with Fellow Pilgrims**: Many pilgrims form strong bonds during their journey. Staying in touch with people you met along the way can help keep the Camino alive for you. Whether it's through social media, reunions, or group chats, these connections can offer support as you transition back to daily life.

- **Living the Camino Values:** The Camino teaches us many things—patience, simplicity, gratitude, and perseverance. These values can be hard to maintain in the hustle of everyday life, but finding ways to incorporate them can help keep the spirit of the Camino alive. Maybe it's as simple as taking more walks, slowing down to appreciate the world around you, or practicing gratitude more intentionally.

Rekindling the Camino Spirit

It's common for pilgrims to feel a pull to return to the Camino after they've gone home. Some pilgrims decide to walk the

Camino Portugués again, while others explore different routes, like the Camino Francés, the Camino del Norte, or even lesser-known paths like the Via de la Plata.

If you find yourself longing for the simplicity of the Camino, consider planning future pilgrimages, either on a different route or the same one. Many pilgrims return again and again, drawn to the experience for reasons they may not fully understand themselves. The Camino has a way of calling people back.

Alternatively, if returning to the Camino isn't immediately possible, you can look for ways to bring the Camino mindset into your life. Volunteering at a pilgrim's albergue or offering help to those planning their own Camino can be a way to give back and stay connected to the community.

Bringing the Camino Home with You

The Camino Portugués isn't just a physical journey. It's an experience that changes you in ways that aren't always obvious at first. As you settle back into daily life, you might notice how the Camino's lessons begin to subtly shape your actions and decisions. Maybe you find yourself more patient, or perhaps you're more open to change. You might appreciate the small things a little more or find yourself craving the simplicity that the Camino brought to your life.

As you pack away your gear, hang up your Compostela, and settle back into your routine, remember that the Camino isn't over. It's still with you, in every choice you make and every step you take forward. You're carrying the spirit of the Camino home with you, and that's something you'll always have, no matter where life takes you next.

Conclusion

As your journey along the **Camino Portugués** reaches its final steps, you arrive at the gates of Santiago de Compostela, where the echoes of pilgrims past linger in the streets, the air, and the ancient stones of the city. The Camino is far more than the distance covered; it's a deeply personal pilgrimage that touches both the heart and soul. For centuries, this path has been walked by all kinds of people—nobles and humble travelers alike, each leaving behind a part of themselves while taking away something far greater.

The Camino teaches us resilience, humility, and the joy of simplicity. On your way, you've crossed breathtaking landscapes, charming towns, and met people whose stories and companionship became an unexpected treasure. You've faced physical challenges and moments of pure joy, found peace in reflection, and shared laughter and camaraderie with fellow pilgrims. Every experience along the trail has added layers to your journey, shaping your understanding of both yourself and the world around you.

As you depart Santiago de Compostela, you take with you more than the memories or the prized Compostela certificate You carry the lessons of the Camino: the quiet power of perseverance, the deep bond of shared community, and the faith that has seen you through each step. This faith may be in something larger than yourself, or simply in the kindness of those you've met, and perhaps even in the strength you've discovered within.

Though your journey on the Camino ends here, its effects will carry on long after you return home. The rhythm of walking, the simplicity of life on the trail, and the sense of purpose with each step—these things can stay with you, influencing your choices, your perspective, and your appreciation for life. You may find that the Camino has changed you in ways you never imagined, bringing a fresh outlook to your daily routines and a deeper understanding of what it means to walk your own path.

Remember, the Camino Portugués is not just a route to Santiago, but a journey that touches the soul. Whether you walked for adventure, personal reflection, or spiritual growth, the lessons you've learned are now a part of you. As you step back into the world beyond the Camino, carry with you its spirit—the sense of wonder, the quiet wisdom, and the connection to something bigger than yourself.

Buen Camino, and may the road ahead be just as meaningful and transformative as the one you've walked.

Made in the USA
Columbia, SC
17 April 2025

56787503R00126